JACKSON FAMILY VALUES

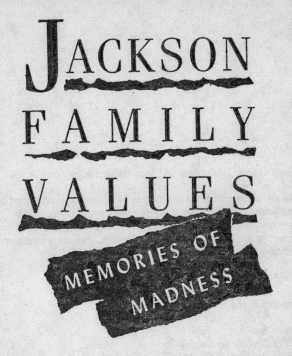

JACKSON FAMILY VALUES

MEMORIES OF MADNESS

Margaret Maldonado Jackson
with Richard Hack

DOVE BOOKS

ISBN 0-7871-1077-9

Printed in the United States of America

Dove Books
8955 Beverly Boulevard
West Hollywood, CA 90048

Distributed by Penguin USA

Cover design and layout by Peter Davis
Text design and layout by Folio Graphics, Inc.
Photo insert by Mauna Eichner

First Mass Market Printing: September 1996

10 9 8 7 6 5 4 3 2 1

ACKNOWLEDGMENTS

My sincere thanks to Michael Viner and Deborah Raffin for allowing me to tell my story through my co-writer, Richard Hack. Richard, you have a gift. Thank you for sharing it with me.

To Army Archerd, for helping the pieces fall into place; Jeanne Viner Bell, for your patience and understanding; Robert Deaton, for cracking the whip and keeping the book on schedule; Jacquie Melnick, for tirelessly transcribing interview tapes; Suzanne de Passe, for being such a positive role model to me; and Tony Jones, for your words of support and elephantine memory. And thanks to my best friend, Anita Camarata, who has never let me down. I love you.

Thank you to Jeremy and Jourdynn. You are the two most important people in my life. To Mommy and Willie and Cy, thank you for never giving up on me, and to Dad, thank you for your prayers.

I want to thank Heidi, for being so loyal; Howard Grossman, for always being there to tell me the bottom line; Joel and Kane Katz, whose friendship has meant a lot to me; Carme Tanuta, for her friendship; Hazel Gordy Jackson, who has grown along with me; and DeeDee Jackson, whose untimely death robbed the world of a special person. I miss you still.

And to the Jackson family, my thanks for teaching me what's really important in life. I hope that someday you'll discover it, too.

For my children, Jeremy and Jourdynn, with love from Mom

—M.M.J.

To my sister Joan, who raised three great kids despite the effects of a deadbeat dad

—R.H.

PROLOGUE

December 11, 1993.

Freedom.

The word motivated me down the second-floor hallway of the Jackson family home in Encino, California. I was making my final exit.

My children, Jeremy and Jourdynn, bounced down the grand staircase, excitedly watching the movers carry out the few belongings we could call our own.

I was turning my back on what many people might think was an incredible lifestyle: living with Jermaine Jackson, the father of my two children, and America's premiere family of pop, sharing all the wonderful perks that fame and fortune had brought them.

They were partly right; that much was fun. So

was having an instant family, one so large you didn't need outside friendships. Rebbie, Jackie, Tito, Jermaine, LaToya, Marlon, Michael, Janet, Randy, and their parents, Katherine and Joseph, had been my family. Their success had been my success, their sorrow, my sorrow.

That was all over now.

DeeDee Jackson, Tito's former wife, warned me that once you escape from the Jackson family circle, the doors close, the gates lock, and you don't go back.

I knew I would be ostracized the way the other spouses had been, but I was past caring. I had been abused and humiliated and my children had been subjected to mental and physical cruelty. We had to leave.

I'd met my common-law husband, Jermaine, soon after the Jacksons' *1984 Victory* tour, a triumph in which each of the brothers would bring home in excess of $5 million. I became a part of the Jackson's world, one that would include hit albums, a TV miniseries, and trips around the world, as well as Ferraris, Rolls-Royces, designer clothing, jewelry, cooks, gardeners, pool men, housekeepers, and enough security guards to ensure the safety of all the above.

The Jacksons' American dream had become

my dream. I was seduced by their sense of family and had yet to learn the ugly secrets behind the facade.

What I saw at first was a mother who loved her children and had managed to keep her famous family together and totally drug free, and a no-nonsense father who was the driving force behind their early success and was now enjoying the fruits of his labor and the rewards of his discipline.

It would be years before the illusion of this "perfect" family would be exposed by the harsh reality of physical threats, mental abuse, lonely nights, and extramarital affairs. I would be lied to, then alternately talked about or ignored.

Having made my escape, I can now tell the story of the Jackson family. My story. The true story.

JACKSON FAMILY VALUES

I hope you're happy. You've split up our family!" Jermaine screamed over the telephone the day after I had left the Jackson compound and was in my new apartment.

It had taken less than twenty-four hours for Jermaine's tears of sadness to turn into an outpouring of rage.

I couldn't believe what he was saying. I had waited all my life for a family I could count on and it had taken Jermaine and his relatives to teach me I could count only on myself. But any anger I felt at him quickly faded as I looked down at the two small, sweet faces before me. Jermaine had given me my children, Jeremy and Jourdynn, the most precious people in my life.

I was born Margaret Marie Maldonado on

February 21, 1965, in Los Angeles. Italian on my mother's side, Mexican on my dad's. Exactly one year, one day, and one hour later, my brother, Willie, was born, just as my parents were in the process of getting a divorce. They were both still teenagers.

My father, Bill, worked in a pizza parlor. After he left us he became a born-again Christian, remarried, and moved to Oregon. My earliest memories of my mother, Joan, are of a woman with an unbridled spirit, a young, carefree, gentle girl-woman who had difficulty assuming responsibility for the two children she had created. By the time I turned six, she was remarried to a man about thirty years her senior. We all moved into his house in the Hollywood Hills.

Cy Gius was a decent, caring man who took over the reins of our care and development. He had children of his own but welcomed Willie and me warmly into his family. At the same time my mother decided to return to school and enrolled at UCLA with a major in philosophy and French. She used her studies as an excuse to travel, and she was gone more often than she was around. I missed her when she was away, but when she was home, I was frankly embarrassed by her. She was a hippie in a strait-laced neighborhood. I'd plead with her to be more like the other moms who dressed conservatively, drove their kids to school, and were active in the PTA. The more I tried to change her, the more she stayed away from home.

Before long, it was Cy who was making our lunches, waking us up every morning, and making certain we did our homework. Even so, my brother and I grew up without many boundaries. Although Cy tried to enforce a strict set of house rules, I began to rebel.

As I left elementary school and entered seventh grade, I started running around with an older wild crowd of teenagers. By the time I turned thirteen, I was drinking and doing drugs, first marijuana and then whatever pills were around. My stepfather was concerned about my behavior and tried to get me back on track, but no one could tell me what to do. I was reckless, stubborn, and determined to live life on my own terms. I started skipping classes and felt I had little in common with my schoolmates. Even though my older friends did some risky things and got into trouble with the police, their world seemed exciting to me.

I struck up a relationship with sixteen-year-old Scotty Wilson, the son of Dennis Wilson of the Beach Boys. His father supplied us with drugs and transportation so we could skip school. One day Scotty and I wandered, happily stoned, into a used clothing store where, on a lark, we attempted to shoplift. Naturally, we were caught.

Not knowing any better, I was pretty charged up and excited about "getting caught"—that is, until I was taken to Central Juvenile Hall in downtown Los Angeles. It was a rough place and smelled like a sewer. I was sure Cy would arrive shortly to get me out of there, but he had decided to teach me a lesson. He let me stay for three days. I was scared. The experience made such an impression on me that afterward I went back to school and tried to focus on my studies. Despite my efforts, I still felt out of step with everyone around me. The urge to rebel was irresistible. I wanted out.

I thought my stepfather's attempts to "control" me were too restricting, so right after I turned sixteen I left home and moved in with an older girlfriend who lived in a guest house at the top of Woodrow Wilson Drive, off Mulholland. It had been a stressful time. My mother and Cy were splitting up, and my brother had decided to stay with Cy. For Willie, it was a smart move. He respected the authority my stepfather imposed and as a result matured from a good kid into a wonderful and talented adult.

I took a different route. After burning out on

the L.A. scene, I sold some belongings and scraped up enough money to buy a plane ticket to New York. No one tried to stop me.

The only one I knew in New York was a friend of mine from L.A. who was now living in White Plains. As soon as I hit *that* town, I knew it wasn't for me. Manhattan was a different story. I fell in love with New York City as soon as I arrived, dazzled by its brilliant lights and infectious energy.

Some friends fixed me up on a blind date with a man named Steve Hayman. I didn't know he was thirty-something with two kids and an ex-wife, and he certainly didn't know I was sixteen. The poor guy thought he was getting a hot date, and he almost lost it when he found out how young I was. He turned out to be a decent guy and remains a good friend to this day. Once he figured out my situation, he set me up in a guest room in Regency House apartments, on Lexington and 63rd and helped me get a job in a clothing store nearby.

I was making a lot of new friends, including a beautiful young woman named Rebecca James, who initiated me into the world known as Studio 54. Even in Los Angeles, I had heard of the world-famous disco with its private VIP room and reputation for heavy drug trafficking. The place didn't disappoint me. It became one of my favorite hangouts.

One thing was guaranteed about my Manhattan adventure: If you're young, attractive, and available, there's going to be a slick mover waiting just for you. For me it was Johnny Calvani, who was Italian, rich, and well connected, with a wealth of celebrity friends, Jack Nicholson among them. He supported his expensive tastes with his restaurant and clothing businesses. I met him one evening at his restaurant and we soon became good friends.

During this period I had almost no contact with my family except for an occasional call to my mother, to whom I would brag about how I had met this celebrity or that one. She'd say, "That's nice," and hang up.

In my own mind I was becoming a big shot, and my world was about to get more exclusive and the treatment more royal. Adnan Khashoggi, the international arms merchant, was about to enter my life. He saw me having dinner one night with a group of friends at Mr. Chow's in Manhattan and sent a bottle of wine to our table. I smiled a thank-you in his direction. He must have liked what he saw, because the bottle of wine was followed by an invitation to a dinner party several nights later at his penthouse in the

Olympic Towers. It was an enormous place, filled with expensive furniture, plush Oriental carpets, crystal and brass chandeliers, and some of the most attractive people in New York City. One of the most beautiful was actress Farrah Fawcett, who had just left the TV show "Charlie's Angels" to embark on a film career.

I felt like a princess in the midst of this crowd and, as the weeks went by, I maneuvered myself into the center of Khashoggi's circle. The relationship with Khashoggi was never sexual. He seemed to be a man who could have had any woman he wanted and didn't push himself on any of them. Instead, he liked to surround himself with beautiful things, and attractive women were just part of the picture.

I was invited back with regularity. Anything I wanted was provided, be it clothes, drugs, or jewelry. Khashoggi gave me a gorgeous matching set of diamond-and-ruby earrings and a ring from Van Cleef & Arpels. I didn't know enough or care enough to be impressed.

I flew in Khashoggi's private jet anywhere in the world I wanted. As the trips increased, so did my fear that maybe Khashoggi wanted more than smiles in return for his generosity. Since I wasn't interested in having sex with the man, I decided to create a distraction. On my next trip—a shopping spree in Paris—I invited four of my girlfriends from Los Angeles to join me. I probably would have never taken the trip, except I was interested in seeing French actor Alain Delon's son, Anthony, who was the most handsome guy I'd ever seen. We had met and had dinner on one of my previous excursions to Paris and I was anxious to pick up where we had left off. Unfortunately for me, I found out Anthony had since struck up a relationship with Princess Stephanie of Monaco. Disappointment didn't even begin to describe the way I felt.

After our Paris shopping spree, my friends and I got back on Khashoggi's jet and headed for Las Palmas, his compound in Spain. The first night there, we all dressed for dinner in our newly purchased Dior gowns. Each of us discovered a ring with a smallish ruby in it on our dinner plates. I remember wondering if Khashoggi kept a box full of the rings somewhere in the house. My girlfriends had a different reaction. They were over the moon at the attention that was being paid to them. Their excitement wasn't lost on Khashoggi, who pointed at one of my friends as we danced and said, "I like that one."

It was the moment of truth and I began to panic. When he added, "Have her come to my room later tonight," I knew I was trapped.

Later in the evening, when I told my friend about Khashoggi's request, her response was "Not in this lifetime," or words to that effect. There was no way she was going to do it. Not wanting to insult him, I went to Khashoggi and told him I hadn't asked her to do it because I wanted to be with him myself. It was a long night for me, but I liked Khashoggi and he had been wonderful to me.

After Khashoggi there were other men and other excesses. My life was one of blurred images, wild nights, and occasional overdoses, all of which I tried to erase from my memory. I was out of control and needed a friend, so I reached out to Johnny Calvani. Despite his reputation as a party guy, I thought Johnny and I could get into a relationship that might be lasting. My timing was bad. He was going to move to L.A. to become a rock star. Grasping for a rope to pull me out of Khashoggi's world, I decided to go with him. We rented a house in the Hollywood Hills. I had come full circle.

I began using more and more drugs. The result was an overdose. Then another. And another. Eventually Johnny became fed up with my substance abuse and gave one of my friends money to get me into a rehabilitation program. He might just as well have spent it on ice and left it to melt on the freeway. No one goes into rehab until he or she is ready, and at that point I wasn't finished with drugs. Instead of getting help, I moved back temporarily into my mother's place. She had yet to deal with her own problems and was in no position to help me. I spent time hanging out with my dealer buddy, getting high on his drugs.

One day I did too many. By the time a friend found me, blood was coming out of my mouth and my eyes had rolled up into their sockets. Paramedics took me to the hospital, struggling to keep me alive. My memory of that day is spotty, but one thing I remember vividly is my brother arriving at the emergency room. He took one look at me on the gurney and was repulsed by what he saw.

"You're throwing your life away, Margaret, and I hate you for it," he said to me. He was crying.

My brother had never talked to me like that before. He was the only one with whom I had any sort of family connection and his words were devastating. I didn't want to think about losing my brother. I decided I would get help and quit drugs. And I did.

The following week I entered a drug rehabilitation program with money from my stepfather. It didn't matter to him that he and my mother were no longer husband and wife. Once again he proved to be a wonderful, generous, and caring man. I owe him my life.

The rehab house I entered was called Tumest, located in Venice, California. It's a tough place that caters to hardened drugs addicts. I fit the bill.

Fear. Solitude. Honesty. Those three words bring back the memory of those months at Tumest. The fear of being in a house full of strangers, all rehabilitating drug addicts, is as horrifying as it is unifying. You seek out friendly faces but aren't allowed to talk.

In Tumest silence is mandatory outside of the regularly scheduled group therapy sessions, which were the reward for good behavior. Punishment meant doing time on the funk squad, where you were denied the right to eat with others or attend group therapy. Funk squad duty might include getting down on your hands and knees and scrubbing the floors with a toothbrush. I did funk squad duty only once and it was more than enough.

After going through Tumest, I thought I might be good at working with troubled kids but, before I could turn that corner in my life, I knew I had to become centered and self-sufficient. I moved in with my stepsister Laura in Venice and got a job. I had gone from the lifestyles of the rich and famous to making the best tuna sandwich on the Venice boardwalk.

I had a couple of good friends who were as happy for me as they were protective. They felt I was in a transition period in which the old temptations might pull me back into that black hole of drugs and despair I had called home for the past five or six years. They kept me busy with stay-at-home dinners and an occasional movie. My strongest supporter and watchdog was a woman named Michelle Lang, who had lobbied Tumest to accept me into their program. She'd convinced the people there that if I didn't get help I would die. Another woman, Keddy Gonzales, had been my friend since childhood. The two of them stuck to me like glue.

On January 17, 1986, my life was about to take another turn. I was almost twenty-one, and it had been about four months since I had gotten out of rehab. Keddy was about to turn twenty-five. She wanted to celebrate with dinner at a restaurant called Bistango's on La Cienega Boulevard in West Hollywood. It sounded like fun. There was, however, some trepidation for all of us. I was nervous about going out on the town for the first time since rehab. My friends were concerned that I might run into some characters from my past life who would be only too eager to pull me back into the fast lane. We decided to give it a shot anyway and off we went.

The place was packed and, as we were waiting for our table, a server came over and said that someone at a nearby table wanted to meet me. Michelle couldn't believe it. We hadn't been in the restaurant two minutes and I was getting hit on. Before I could say a word, she told the server on my behalf, "Thanks, but no thanks."

A minute later a short Italian man walked our way and tried the same routine: "A friend of mine would really like to meet you," he said to me as Michelle again jumped in to intervene.

"Look," she said to the guy, gently pushing him away, "we're celebrating a birthday. We're here to have dinner, nothing more! Go away."

So much, I thought, for the interested guy. Little did I know.

"Hi," came a soft voice from behind me, almost drowned out by the din around us. I turned and found myself facing an attractive black man wearing a ridiculous white leather jacket with shoulder pads that looked like it had come from the wardrobe department of "Star Trek." I said hello and could see my girlfriends about to tell this guy to get lost when another server stepped between us. He told the man that some girls were asking for his autograph. They both went off and I figured that was that.

I didn't think a whole lot about it until he came over to me again later. At this point I knew he must be someone famous. In that jacket I thought he might be one of the Commodores.

"I saw you signing autographs," I said, trying not to appear star struck. "Who are you, anyway?" He said he was "one of the Jacksons." It was not until later that I found out he was Jermaine.

During the course of our dinner, I could see him staring our way, but my attention remained focused on Keddy. After all, it was her birthday. Still, as a child I had grown up listening to the Jackson 5 on my Pinocchio record player, so I allowed myself to sneak a few curious peeks at him as well.

Jermaine quickly made a deal with the restaurant to pick up the cost of Keddy's cake and, near the end of our meal, he reappeared at our table to serenade the birthday girl. He started telling me about a music video he was going to be shooting and asked if I'd like to be in it. I said I would, so he took my phone number and said someone might give me a call sometime.

The "someone" turned out to be him. The "sometime" turned out to be the following morning at nine. I never got to be in a video.

I hadn't expected Jermaine to call me or even to save my number. But on January 18, 1986, the morning after our first meeting, I answered the phone and heard the sound of his voice.

We had a telephone courtship for the first two weeks. He told me about his new record, his plans, and his dreams, and seemed interested in what I had to say. You learn in rehab to be honest about your life, so I was entirely open with him about my past and my hopes for a drug-free future. I couldn't imagine what he was thinking, hearing about my overdoses and fast life, since I thought none of the Jacksons had ever tried drugs.

I later realized that wounded or needy women

are ideal for Jackson men—they're dependent and easy to control—but at the time all I could see was that he was showing an honest interest in the fact that I had turned my life around. That impressed me.

He talked about his brothers and his parents with such affection that he made his life seem fairy-tale perfect. He had everything I had ever hoped for except the white picket fence. The Jacksons had a twelve-foot-high iron gate backed by security guards. Close enough for me.

The more I heard, the more I liked. He told me about growing up in Gary, Indiana, sleeping with all his brothers in bunk beds stacked in a tiny bedroom. He said there wasn't much money but the kids always felt rich because of the closeness of the family. I was fascinated by the Jacksons' earlier lives and how involved their parents, Joseph and Katherine, were in the success of the children. It was a long way from the way I'd grown up.

Every day this wonderful, soft, seductive voice would come on the phone and we would talk, laugh, and share experiences. Even though I had seen him only once, I felt that he was becoming a significant person in my life.

Jermaine never gave me his phone number and I didn't ask for it. As it turned out, that wasn't the only thing I didn't know about him. In each conversation Jermaine would allude to something he wanted to reveal to me but wouldn't over the telephone.

Flowers, chocolates, and sweet notes filled my room. It was fun getting up every day wondering what surprise Jermaine might send my way. I later learned that he had romanced Whitney Houston, the beautiful model Iman, and Stevie Wonder's sister. He had courtship down pat.

My stepsister didn't share my enthusiasm for my famous suitor. When I told her about Jermaine's phone calls and presents, she rolled her eyes and gave me that won't-you-ever-learn look. "I think he's married, Margaret," she told me. "I think he's married to Berry Gordy's daughter. You know, the guy who founded Motown Records."

The next time Jermaine called I asked about his marital status. He told me his marriage to Hazel Gordy Jackson was the secret he hadn't wanted to tell me over the phone.

"I wanted to explain this in the right way, Margaret," he said, his voice softer than ever. "I've been married since I was nineteen and I have two children, Jermaine Jr. and Autumn Joy." After a pause he added, "It's over though, Margaret. We're planning on getting a divorce.

We're only waiting until the end of the school year for the children. The separation will be official by the end of summer."

He sounded so sad and hurt as he told me all this that I felt both relieved and guilty about being angry. He was putting the feelings of his children before his own, and that endeared him to me.

Jermaine said his wife, Hazel, no longer needed him and was no longer content just to be his wife. He said they had gotten married too young, had started a family too soon, and had grown into different people as they had matured. Their love was gone; their marriage was finished. "We don't even live together anymore," he added, saying that he had moved into the guest house on their Brentwood property while Hazel remained with the children in the main house.

A few days and many phone calls later, Jermaine invited me to come to the LionShare recording studio. When I got there the place was empty except for his engineer. Jermaine was recording the song "Turning Your Words into Action," which would be released later that year. As I watched him work and listened to the music, I thought, *I'm falling in love*.

When he came out of the recording booth and asked me what I thought of the song, I was on a high from all the excitement and energy. I don't remember what I said, but I remember what I felt. My heart was thumping wildly, and I was thrilled just to be near him. We were both a little shy with each other. It was nice. After he was finished at the studio, we got into his limo and drove north on Pacific Coast Highway to a little beach town and back again. He held my hand the whole time and listened to every word I said. I felt wonderful and he looked happy.

In the following weeks I saw Jermaine often. I was amazed that each time he picked me up at my house he seemed to be driving a different car. He had a Ferrari one day, a Rolls-Royce the next. He was probably trying to impress me. At the time I thought he knew a lot about cars.

I mentioned some of my future plans, telling him my intentions to move in with some friends and buy a car. Jermaine offered to help me out by renting a car for me for a few weeks. I thought that was sweet and he seemed to want to do it. I expected a VW Rabbit; what I got was a Mercedes-Benz.

Moving into the large house in Westwood with two centered, working women—one a violin teacher, the other in real estate—gave me my first true taste of how wonderful life on my own could be. Together we shared a genuine all-for-one attitude that made even the most mundane task seem like fun. Jermaine joined in the spirit of things, endearing himself to my roommates. They thought he was adorable. He would pop by with presents and was quick to help when we made an effort to fix the place up. I soon learned that while Jermaine may have had a lot of special qualities, a handyman he was not. He made up for it in so many other ways that, as the weeks progressed, I began accepting the fact that I was in love with him.

I went on the road with him during the promotional tour for his new album *Precious Moments*. The tour took us to Canada and all over the United States. Jermaine traveled with a trio of regulars: Flip Wilson's son Kevin, a guy named Franco (who turned out to be the short Italian who approached us at Bistango's), and an Israeli security guard who was trained in martial arts and guerrilla warfare.

One person who never seemed to be in the picture was Jermaine's wife, Hazel. He never called her when I was around, he didn't refer to her, and her name was never even brought up by those in his entourage. Even if someone had talked about her I probably wouldn't have heard it. I was too happy. Jermaine had told me he loved me for the first time.

At last my life was on track. I had put drugs behind me and found a stable, gentle man with whom I thought I could raise a family and live happily ever after. He told me he wanted to marry me and that he wanted a baby to start our life together. At the time there was nothing he would have said that I wouldn't have believed. Later I learned that pregnancies are one of the ways through which many of the Jackson men control their women. Contrary to the popular notion, their wives, common-law wives, and girlfriends may not have had to go barefoot, but they often were kept pregnant.

I found out I was pregnant on Mother's Day 1986, and I was thrilled. In the back of my mind, I began painting that picture of the white picket fence. There would be a nice home in the hills with a new baby and a husband who loved children, didn't do drugs, hated going to clubs, and wasn't interested in other women. The fact that he had been married for thirteen years to the same woman only reinforced my belief in his monogamy. I thought he'd just gotten married too young.

Jermaine seemed delighted with my pregnancy and went around announcing the news to anyone who would listen. We had been seeing each other for seven months, and his legal separation from Hazel was well under way. Or so I thought.

I had moved out of the place I shared with my two roommates to house-sit for a friend who was in the south of France for several months. While I was house-sitting, a longtime girlfriend, Kim, was having some problems, so I invited her to stay with me for a few days. One night, when she returned from a late dinner with some friends, she seemed upset. After I coaxed and pleaded, the news came tumbling out.

"Jermaine isn't separated from his wife. He's happily married. I'm a good friend of Hazel's two brothers, Berry and Kennedy," Kim said. "I know what I'm talking about, Margaret."

"You're crazy," I laughed. "He and Hazel don't even talk. He lives in the guest house on the property, but that's it."

"Well, if he's living in the guest house, why is his wife pregnant?" she countered.

My mind faded to black. I got angry and directed the anger unnecessarily at Kim, telling her to get out of the house and stay as far away from me as possible. I was seven months pregnant and didn't want to hear these kinds of lies.

Although Jermaine had been on the road touring for the past several months, that particular night he happened to be in Los Angeles to perform at the Universal Amphitheatre. I had chosen to skip the concert since I knew his entire family would be there. During my pregnancy I had gained eighty-two pounds; not the picture I was anxious to present to them. I had his telephone number, even though I had never used it. This was one time, though, when I decided I needed some answers and needed them fast. By this time it was after midnight and I figured he'd be home from the concert. I dialed the number.

"Hello," a groggy voice answered. I knew it was Hazel and that I must have awakened her.

I asked to speak with Jermaine and, when she inquired, I told her my name. I counted the seconds until Jermaine came on the line. I knew if he was living in the guest house it would take at least a few minutes to get him on the phone. It took less than ten seconds for him to come on. When Jermaine heard what I had to say, he could only plead, "Wait, wait, wait."

I had no trouble speaking at all. "You and your wife aren't separated," I screamed. "You lied to me, Jermaine. I don't want to have a baby with you. I don't know what I'll do, but whatever it is, it's not going to involve you. I don't ever want to see you again!"

I knew Hazel had to be right next to him,

listening to every word, just as I knew I wasn't the only one to whom he'd have to do a lot of explaining.

"Stay with your wife, Jermaine," I said. "That's where you belong. She's pregnant and you have a family with her. I don't want this on my conscience. I can't live with this. So stay where you are and don't ever, ever see me again." I slammed down the phone.

Soon Jermaine was at my door. I was so furious now that I couldn't say anything. He tried to explain. He told me he had fallen in love with me when we first met. He said Hazel had gotten pregnant after she followed him to Hawaii while he was on tour, adding that she would do anything in order to save their marriage.

He insisted they were still going to separate and continued repeating that the marriage was over in his mind, even though it hadn't happened yet. I accused him again of lying to me.

"What was I supposed to do?" he asked. "If I told you the truth, you would have left. I could see where you were going in your life. The last thing you needed was another mess." Unfortunately, he hit the nail right on the head. That was exactly what I faced. I still had feelings for Jermaine but what he had done was irresponsible and unconscionable. I felt badly for Hazel and even worse for myself.

The next day Jermaine called and, after asking how I was feeling, told me he was continuing on his tour and heading out of the state. There was a new nervousness in his voice that suggested he was unsure which direction our relationship would go. He did, however, assure me that he planned on taking care of both the baby and me. He told me to look for an apartment and said he'd take care of the expense. It was several weeks before I saw Jermaine again. During that time I had a realtor friend show me a few small apartments.

This was not a happy time for me. I was nearly eight months pregnant, uncomfortable and completely unsure of my future. When Jermaine returned to Los Angeles, I showed him several apartments I thought were acceptable, but he didn't like any of them. Every place I showed him was "too small" or "in the wrong neighborhood."

He eventually selected a three-bedroom condominium in Pacific Palisades for $2,000 a month and plunked down an entire year's rent in advance. Jermaine also suggested I hire a nanny and housekeeper. He referred me to a woman named Nellie, who turned out to be wonderful. About three weeks before I was due to give birth, I moved into the new condo.

Jermaine took me to a children's furniture

store and practically bought out the place. All I had in mind was a nice wooden crib and a bassinet. What I got was a brass canopy bed with a matching dresser and bassinet—and that was just the beginning. The condo was soon filled with baby furniture.

As my delivery date neared, I saw Jermaine about twice a week. He was so anxious for the baby to come that he and I would go for long walks trying to induce labor. The walks gave us time to talk. He kept reassuring me that his relationship with Hazel was a thing of the past. I'd look at him, not knowing what to believe anymore. I was grateful for the support he was giving me, even though this wasn't the relationship I had dreamed of but, under the circumstances, I knew things could have been a lot worse.

On the day before Christmas, I began to feel what I thought were labor pains. I was all alone and didn't know what to do, so I telephoned my doctor. He told me to get to Cedars-Sinai Medical Center, which was a good thirty minutes away from my Palisades condo.

As I drove myself to the hospital, I felt sharp cramps, which intensified my anxiety. But when I arrived at the hospital emergency room, the doctors sent me home, saying I was only beginning the birth process and hadn't begun labor.

Back at home the intensity of the cramps became so bad I could hardly breathe. I figured these *had* to be labor pains. I got back in my car and made a second trip alone to the hospital. Again, they said the real labor hadn't started and told me to return home. By this time I was exhausted from the trips to and from the hospital. I swore there would be no more false alarms and went to bed.

On Christmas Day the sensation I was feeling went from gripping cramps to intense pain and I called my mother. I needed someone with experience to stay with me. To my relief, she came over right away.

On the next trip to the hospital, my mother decided it was a good time for an argument. She kept asking why Jermaine wasn't with us. In truth, Jermaine was home with his two children and pregnant wife enjoying a family Christmas. He knew I was going into labor. I had called to tell him before each trip I made to the hospital and he hadn't come. I didn't see why he would come now. I knew the horrible predicament I had gotten myself into and didn't need to be reminded about it. The more anxious I got listening to my mother, the worse my labor pains became.

When we got to the hospital, I was doubled

over in so much pain I couldn't talk in complete sentences. I was having trouble breathing and was rushed into the emergency room. I couldn't believe it when the doctor announced I was insufficiently dilated and sent me home again.

My mother drove me back, keeping up her tirade about Jermaine's absence. I finally asked her to leave. When she did, the reality of my situation hit me. I was alone physically, emotionally, and financially. This was not the ideal frame of mind in which to be experiencing the contractions of labor. I wouldn't recommend it to anyone.

I was not comforted by the knowledge that, not far away at his Brentwood estate, Jermaine was finishing unwrapping presents with his family and was preparing to take them all to a holiday dinner at the home of his longtime friends, singer Pia Zadora and her then-husband, billionaire Meshulam Riklis. If he was concerned about my delivery, it wasn't obvious to me.

As the day progressed, I did speak with Jermaine, who said, in typical Jackson fashion, that he had arranged for a limousine to take me to the hospital when the time came. Since I thought the time had come and gone three times already, I was not about to go back to the hospital for a fourth time on a false alarm.

Finally, in the early evening, my labor was so intense that I called the car service. I also called my brother, Willie. A few minutes later a driver was at my door helping me toward a black Lincoln stretch limousine. It was quite a scene: me in the back of a limo in excruciating pain, with a total stranger driving up front. He was sweating as much as I was. The poor guy was so nervous, he sped all the way to the hospital, dodging traffic and ignoring red lights. When we got there, everyone kept trying to give him forms to fill out. They all thought he was the father.

This time the doctors didn't send me home and I was wheeled into the maternity wing. Fifteen hours later I gave birth to my first beautiful baby, Jeremy Maldonado Jackson. Because I didn't know how things were going to work out with Jermaine, I wanted my son to have Maldonado as his middle name so he would also keep my identity. In my mind I knew there was a good probability that I was going to raise this child entirely on my own.

My brother had arrived at the hospital a few minutes after I did and was there with me through the entire ordeal. Jermaine had called the hospital from Pia Zadora's house and Willie told him if he wanted to be there in time for the birth he should leave right away. Jermaine, I found out later from Pia, had turned the Christmas feast into a fiasco, excusing himself from the table every twenty minutes for an update on the birth of his baby, while his pregnant wife tried to hold a normal conversation with Meshulam and Pia.

Jeremy was born in the early morning hours of December 26, 1986. Jermaine did manage to make it to the hospital about an hour before the actual delivery and joined my brother alongside me for the event. Given the drama that had preceded the birth, the actual delivery went smoothly and without complications. After a day in the hospital, Jermaine took Jeremy and me back to the condo in Pacific Palisades, leaving us as soon as he saw we were safely back home.

Although my future was uncertain, I was deliriously happy. In spite of all I had put my body through in my teenage years, Jeremy had been born a perfectly beautiful, healthy baby. Even if nothing else wonderful happened for the rest of my life, at that moment I knew I was the happiest woman on Earth.

3

As the new year progressed, Jermaine began coming to the condo more and more often. He loved holding Jeremy. While I watched them play, I couldn't help thinking that under different circumstances, Jermaine would have made an excellent dad. He was so proud of his infant son that in mid-March I wasn't surprised when Jermaine asked to be allowed to take Jeremy to Marlon's thirtieth birthday party at the Bistro Garden. I knew other members of his family would be there, but I hadn't realized a lot of show business people were also invited and that Jermaine would be attending with his pregnant wife.

Although I still didn't know if Jermaine and I would eventually live together, I wanted my son to meet his father's family and the party seemed like a good opportunity. To make Jeremy's introduction perfect, my housekeeper, Nellie, and I designed a little velvet tuxedo for him and he looked absolutely adorable in it.

As father and son entered the private room of the posh Beverly Hills restaurant, cameras clicked. Jermaine was carrying Jeremy and proudly introducing him around the room. The following week a photo of Jeremy ran in the *National Enquirer* under the headline JERMAINE JACKSON'S LOVE CHILD. The article announced that Jermaine had shown up at the event with his new son as well as his wife of thirteen years, who was due to give birth in about one week.

I was angry that Jermaine would allow our child to be exploited that way. I felt even worse for Hazel, who must have been humiliated by her husband carrying around someone else's baby when she herself was so obviously pregnant. The guest list included Lionel Richie and Kenny Rogers. I could only imagine what they must have thought.

I told Jermaine how I felt about it and he tried to place the blame on Marlon's wife, Carol. He said that Carol had sold the photograph to the *Enquirer* to embarrass Jermaine. Jermaine claimed that Carol had had a crush on him before she met Marlon. He said she had once held up a banner at a Jackson 5 concert proclaiming I LOVE YOU JERMAINE. She supposedly gave him her phone number after the show and Jermaine gave it to Marlon. Even though Marlon ended up marrying Carol, she never forgave Jermaine for passing her on to his brother. At least, that's the story Jermaine told me.

Not long after that, Jermaine said everyone in the family loved Jeremy so much that he wanted to take him to a family softball game. I knew the Jackson brothers played in the show business league with other entertainers so I said Jeremy could go.

The day went by slowly as I waited for Jeremy to come home. As afternoon began to stretch into early evening, I got worried and called Jermaine's home number for the second time. Once again Hazel answered the phone. I identified myself and said I was wondering if she knew where Jeremy was.

"He's right here with me," she answered, seemingly surprised that I didn't already know. She said Jermaine had left Jeremy with her and went off to play softball with his brothers. I couldn't believe what she was saying. When I explained that it was my understanding that Jermaine had taken Jeremy to be with his family, she answered that Jeremy *was* with his family—meaning Hazel and her kids.

At that point I had never met Hazel and she didn't know me, but the two of us were about to have an interesting conversation. Hazel asked me to hold on while she went to a different telephone, apparently not wanting to talk in front of Jermaine's two older children. When she got back on the line, she hit me with a question that stopped me cold.

"You aren't planning on giving up this baby, are you, Margaret?" she asked.

"Give him up? To whom?" I asked.

"To Jermaine and me," Hazel said, now sounding as upset as I was.

I told her I wasn't about to give Jeremy to anyone; that I had every intention of raising him myself.

Hazel was speechless and I later learned why. Jermaine had convinced her that I didn't want to keep Jeremy and that they should adopt the child and raise him. She not only had agreed but had shopped for two of everything—two bassinets, two cribs, two dressers, two of each outfit she bought, one for Jeremy and one for the child she was carrying.

Her voice sounded shaky when I said I was coming to pick Jeremy up. She said she would see to it that Jeremy was safely returned home. I didn't want to cause any problems for Hazel, who was only days away from giving birth. As far as Jermaine was concerned, however, I wanted an explanation and was not about to let him talk his way out of this one.

When Jermaine brought Jeremy back to the condo, I put the baby to bed and returned to the living room as mad as I've ever been.

"I don't know Hazel," I told Jermaine. "I don't know if she has hostile feelings toward me or my child. And I don't want Jeremy left with someone I don't know." Jermaine could feel the heat and tried another sidestep.

This time he focused the blame on his older children, Jermaine Jr. and Autumn, telling me how excited they were about having a baby brother and how they begged him to bring Jeremy to their house for the day.

This was my Prince Charming? If he'd been Pinocchio he would have been tripping over his own nose.

Jermaine was there on March 17, 1987, when Hazel gave birth to Jaimy, but began spending even more time at the condo with me, playing the good dad.

One day he brought Jaimy over for a visit to meet his half-brother. I was sure he never let

Hazel know that he was bringing Jaimy to my house, just as he did to me when he took Jeremy to his and Hazel's home. The diapers were a dead giveaway. Hazel used Pampers and I used Huggies. When Jaimy needed changing, I used what I had in the house. Hazel had to have noticed the difference. I noticed when Jeremy came back from a ride with Jermaine wearing Pampers in place of his usual Huggies.

Jaimy was an adorable baby with long legs and fingers, and I became quite fond of him. Jaimy and Jeremy began a friendship when they were little that continues today.

Once Jaimy was born, Hazel reassessed her situation and must have decided she didn't need the aggravation of Jermaine in her life. In October 1987, while he was doing a series of concerts in Australia, she filed for divorce and demanded $25,000 a month in alimony, which included $7,500 in child support for her three children. At first he complied and paid what she asked.

Two months earlier, in August 1987, Jermaine's brother Jackie had become the first of the Jackson brothers to get a divorce. His wife, Enid, had caught Jackie having an affair with Paula Abdul. "Caught" probably isn't the right word. Jackie did little to keep it a secret during its long run.

The affair came to a climax one evening in 1984, right before the start of the Jacksons' *Victory* tour. Jackie had taken Paula to the movies at the Sepulveda Drive-In Theater. Marlon's wife, Carol, found out about it and for some reason thought it would be a good idea to tell Enid, even though Enid and Jackie were separated at the time. Enid jumped into Jackie's Mercedes-Benz, drove to the theater, and located Jackie sitting beside Paula in his Range Rover. Enid yanked Paula out of the Range Rover by her hair and dragged her across the theater lot while Jackie tried to pull his wife away. Jackie was still trying to help Paula when Enid got back into the Mercedes. She jammed the car into reverse and ran into Jackie's leg. The broken leg not only ended Jackie's marriage to Enid, but it also kept him from performing on the *Victory* tour. What it didn't do was keep him from collecting his $5 million cut; a fact Jermaine would never let him forget.

Three years later Enid filed for divorce, asking for $40,000 a month in support payments. When the legal smoke cleared, she was awarded $5,000 a month for herself and $3,500 a month for her children, Siggie and Brandy, plus 20 percent of Jackie's income; which amounted to more than a quarter of a million dollars, plus half of the royalties Jackie received on songs he composed during their marriage. As Enid quickly learned, though, winning the judgment is one thing, collecting the funds is another. In the end she would collect just under $200,000 in a settlement.

Then, in September, Enid had Jackie arrested for violating the terms of their divorce. He had come to the sprawling house they once shared (a house previously owned by Rob Reiner and Penny Marshall) and tried to use the recording studio he'd built there. When Enid turned him away, he broke in through the French door leading into the kitchen. Right after the glass hit the floor he was in police custody.

I asked Jermaine about it. He took his brother's side and claimed Enid had provoked the attack. According to Jermaine, he and Jackie were in the recording studio when Enid raced into the room, took off her shoe, and started to beat Jackie; calling him a faggot in front of everyone.

After Hazel threw him out, Jermaine moved in with Jeremy and me. The Jermaine that arrived at the condo was a defeated person. Not only had he been given the boot by his wife, he also had another big surprise to admit to me.

"I only have $300 to my name," he said in the same soft voice he had used when we first met. I couldn't believe what I was hearing. Like all of his brothers, he had made $5 million from the *Victory* tour in 1984, drove around in a Ferrari, and had a huge estate in Brentwood. How could he possibly be broke? I was shocked by what he said but told him not to worry, that we would manage somehow. In some ways I thought it would be better if he was broke so we could get a fresh start.

To generate some quick income, he was booked to perform a show in a stadium in Kenya and wanted me to go with him. I was nervous about leaving Jeremy with his nanny for the first time, even though it was only for a week, but I thought it would give Jermaine and me time to work things out.

The bad news was he never got paid for the concert; the good news was Jermaine and I decided to stay together. When we returned to California, it was as if we were coming back from our honeymoon. We settled into a life as a family and I discovered myself being thrust into the new role of manager. Jermaine's affairs were a mess. Despite the fact that he had received millions for the *Victory* tour, he was deep in debt, particularly to the Internal Revenue Service.

He and Hazel had bought an expensive home and were driving around in expensive cars but had barely enough to pay the light bill. My first order of business was to fire his accountants and bring in new ones to reorganize his debts and his continuing obligations, including Hazel's child support.

I hadn't finished tenth grade and math was not my best subject, but I managed to take what we had coming in and spread it around to the various places I knew it must go. It helped that we had two good people in our corner, Jermaine's lawyer, Joel Katz, and his new business manager, Howard Grossman.

Hazel and Jermaine soon sold their Brentwood estate. More accurately, they were almost pushed out of the neighborhood. When he was living there, Jermaine had had a set of large black-and-gold gates with the initials HGJ and JLJ installed at the front of the estate. The gates looked more appropriate for an embassy than for a family home. They were so garish that horrified neighbors held meetings trying to come up with a legal way to get the gates out of there. Ironically, Jermaine and Hazel's next-door neighbor ended up buying the estate. The gates were taken down by Jermaine and put into storage.

Jermaine moved Hazel into a house in Beverly Hills that cost $25,000 a month to rent. The money from the sale of the estate went to pay back debts, many from the *Precious Moments* tour. Jermaine had borrowed heavily to finance the tour. A smart businessman like Michael would have gotten a sponsor to foot most of the costs, but none came forward for Jermaine, as far as I know. He was so intent on touring and so sure he would be received with as much hoopla as that surrounding the *Victory* tour that he mortgaged his house and picked up the bill himself. The *Precious Moments* album went nowhere and so did the tour.

Jermaine's version is that he was told there would be sponsors. When none came through, he decided to pick up the tab himself. In reality his attorney and his agents begged him not to attempt a solo tour, but some artists hear what they want to hear. What Jermaine wanted to hear was the roar of the fans cheering for him and him alone. It was a sound that was not to be.

After Hazel and Jermaine split, he performed in concert here and there. In the meantime some money was coming in from his record deal with Arista. But his lifestyle far exceeded his income and was a continuing problem. My only luxury was keeping Nellie as a nanny to help with Jeremy. It seemed justified in exchange for the round-the-clock attention Jermaine seemed to require.

The lease was coming up on our condo and, because of the financial drain on Jermaine's income, we decided to move. I found a two-bedroom condo on Wilshire Boulevard in Westwood, right across the street from where Jermaine's brother Randy lived. Compared with our condo, Randy's was a palace. It had black-and-white checkered marble floors and a wonderful curved staircase to the second floor. Jermaine and I were fascinated with the gadgets, including a series of televisions that came out of the floor via a remote control. It was a great bachelor pad. Our place was a typical two-bedroom, two-bath condo with wall-to-wall carpeting and a standard kitchen. I'd sit in our living room and look across the street at Randy's building. I'd watch his girlfriend at the time, a beautiful woman named Bernadette Robi, who is now married to Sugar Ray Leonard, pull her car up to the valet and disappear inside.

Even though Jermaine and I were trying to economize, it was a happy time in my life. I had a child, a man who loved me, and as normal a family life as I had ever experienced. Jermaine seemed to be working hard to meet all his obligations. He was back in the recording studio for his second album for Arista Records, *Two Ships*. At the same time he began working with Randy, Jackie, and Tito on what would be the last

Jacksons album, 2300 *Jackson Street,* for CBS Records. Tito was the one responsible for organizing the album, which was being recorded at Ponderosa, his home-based studio in Encino. Each time I'd drop by the recording sessions I'd meet another brother. Tito always seemed to be in the garage working on his vintage car collection or his favorite model airplanes. His wife, Dee Dee, would playfully snatch Jeremy out of my arms and run around the house romping and laughing with my son and her own. I met Jackie, who was still dating Paula Abdul at the time. He invited Jermaine and me to join them sometime for a movie, which I thought sounded like fun.

Finally I got to meet Katherine. Well, sort of. I saw her in the driveway of Tito's house in her Rolls and waved in her direction. She looked in my direction, looked away, and drove off without waving back. I was hurt but not surprised considering the circumstances.

When I told Jermaine that Jackie had invited us to join Paula and him at the movies, his response was strange. He said, "Be careful what you say to Jackie. I don't want him knowing any of our business." *That's interesting,* I thought to myself. In retrospect the remark should have been my first clue that the brothers didn't trust one another. I'd later find out that the entire family was party to this Jacksonian paranoia.

I got a better sense of the family dynamics when I visited the Jackson compound on Hayvenhurst Drive in Encino for the first time. It was the house that Joseph had purchased for the family in 1971 and which Michael had totally gutted and remodeled ten years later.

It was a rainy day. Jermaine had dropped off Jeremy and me at the compound on the way to Tito's house, where he and his brothers were recording. He said he wanted me to get to know his mother and formally introduced us in the large kitchen of the house. Then he left, and Katherine and I sat down at the kitchen table. I could feel her eyes staring right through me. I tried to make small talk, updating her on Jeremy, but she seemed uncomfortable. Later I figured out that Katherine was seeing in me all the women with whom her husband Joseph had had affairs. During that first meeting, she seemed to warm up a little to me. What she wasn't was accepting. It would be another six months before Katherine would openly welcome me into the family. A very long six months.

Christmas 1987 found Jermaine and me celebrating under a large tree in our Wilshire condo along with Jaimy, Jermaine Jr., and Autumn. Jermaine and I had piled the living room high with gifts for everyone. When Jermaine's other children were with us, I tried to make them feel welcome and at home. I knew what it was like to live with a stepparent, no matter how kind he or she might be, and to feel like a visitor in your own home. I didn't want them to go through that.

I was anxious to get married and Jermaine seemed to be, too, but his divorce wasn't final from Hazel and wouldn't be for several months. Even though Jermaine was continuing to work, it became clear that he wouldn't be able to maintain Hazel's alimony payments. The judgment was changed to one half of the income Jermaine generated.

When Jermaine and I were leaving to go out of the country for a concert, Hazel had us served with subpoenas at the airport. It was a first for me. The process server approached us and took our picture. Then, just like a fan, he handed us a paper as if he wanted an autograph. What he wanted was to tell us we were both served.

It always concerned me that Hazel's father, Berry Gordy, might try to hurt Jermaine professionally, although he never did. Berry was always a gentleman and very fair where Jermaine was concerned. Hazel was another story at first. She was used to living a certain lifestyle and could see it slipping away. Her father hired a private investigator and attorneys in an effort to force

Jermaine to own up to his responsibilities. I don't think she believed things were quite as bad as they were. Whenever she didn't get a check, she would call to complain, usually to me. I felt badly about the situation and made every effort to see that she would always get something, no matter how small the amount.

One day she called and snapped at me, ordering me to see to it that she got a check. I told her that if she intended to use that tone, she needn't bother calling me again. My standing up to her seemed to clear the air and we started a friendship that continues to this day.

Some people can't understand the relationship Hazel and I have, but they haven't stopped to think how much we have in common. The basis of our friendship is our mutual wish for all our children to be happy and well taken care of. It's a strong bond.

Just as things seemed to be settling down for Jermaine and me, the 1987 Whittier earthquake hit. Living in a high-rise condominium didn't seem like such a good idea anymore. By that time both Jermaine and I had begun having long conversations on the phone with Katherine each morning talking about various members of the family. Gossip is a serious art form for the Jackson family. We'd talk about Jackie's latest girlfriend, or the fact that no one could find Randy, or why Marlon and Carol never visited any of the other family members. After the earthquake, all Jermaine could talk about was getting us out of that high-rise.

He suggested we move in with Katherine, Joseph, Michael, and LaToya at the Hayvenhurst house. I loved the idea. Both Joseph and Michael thought that was a great plan; Katherine was another story. She wanted Jermaine to come back home and she liked me fairly well by that time. What she didn't like was the fact that we hadn't gotten married yet. Her religious beliefs were in conflict with her heart. Eventually, her heart won out.

I encouraged the move wholeheartedly. I wanted Katherine to get to know Jeremy and me and I thought that I would be moving into a safe environment. The opportunity to become close to Katherine was a major motivating force for me. She was the mother I had always dreamed of having. When she agreed to allow us to move in, I was elated.

My new address was Hayvenhurst Drive, Encino.

It was going to be the best time of my life.

4

The Jacksons simply call it Hayvenhurst. The family compound in Encino, California, is fronted by large, black wrought-iron gates and a guard house, in which two security people keep watch day and night. Toward the rear of the property is a second security post—a watchtower—from which the entire property can be observed.

As we moved in that sunny winter day in 1988, I took another look around the house, decorated with ornate gold Italianate furniture. The white marble entryway, which had a chandelier that looked like a crystal waterfall, led to the grand stairway, which was covered in thick forest-green carpet. A large grandfather clock and Grecian bronze statues completed the picture.

Katherine had opened up Janet's old room upstairs for Jermaine, Jeremy, and me to use. By that time Janet had moved to a hillside condo with her director-boyfriend, René Elizondo. Her old room wasn't overly large but had a white marble fireplace and a black marble bathroom. It was a step up from our Wilshire Boulevard condo.

Directly across the hall from us was LaToya's room, with its peach carpet and similar white marble fireplace and black marble bath. In the other upstairs wing of the house was Katherine and Joseph's suite, which had its own sitting area and large bath.

At the end of our hallway was Michael's room, the largest in the house. He'd paid to have the house remodeled and added his room, which was two stories high with a winding stairway that led to a balcony with its own Jacuzzi. A private entrance allowed Michael to come and go as he pleased. His room once housed a glass case that held statuettes of the seven dwarfs from Disney's *Snow White*, but it had been moved to the trophy room downstairs. There were pictures of Peter Pan hung on the walls and CDs and tapes scattered all over the floor. Michael had the regulation Jackson black marble bathroom, except his had faucets in the shape of gold swans.

Jermaine looked at it all noncommittally as he showed me around.

I spent my first few days wandering around the property. One of my first and favorite stops was the trophy room, a testimony to the family's extraordinary career. It was lined wall-to-wall with awards, gold records, magazine covers, and citations from governments around the world— some for Michael, some for the Jackson 5.

I would later learn that this room was a sore reminder to the other Jackson brothers of how far Michael's career had outstripped theirs.

At the moment, however, I knew of no trouble in paradise. I was still marveling at the scope of it all. I loved the living room, which Katherine had decorated in soft shades of peach and green. The room had beautiful, thick carpeting, a large, wood-burning fireplace, and a grand piano (which only Randy played) in a corner. Pictures of family members were all around. It was an inviting room but one that was almost never used. The kitchen was the favorite family room, the place where everyone congregated and talked as they sat at the big, round table, a great island in the center of the gleaming white tile floor and black and chrome appliances.

When I first arrived, each of us was on a different schedule, so we all made our own meals. Katherine loved to make greens, pinto beans, homemade chicken soup, and hot-water corn bread. Joseph's favorite was salmon croquettes and fried okra. I loved Italian, of course, so I'd pile on the pasta. Katherine taught me how to make the recipes her children loved, including fried catfish, biscuits, and bacon. My turkey tacos went over pretty well with everyone except Michael, of course. He was a strict vegetarian. He had his own chef, but he seemed to live on rice and beans alone. He is a sugar junkie, however, and eats candy for an energy fix. Any kind of candy. He likes it all.

The real noneater in the house was LaToya. She would go three or four days locked in her room without eating a thing. I figured it was the only way she could fit into the clothes she wore. LaToya went around giving off the impression of a refined young lady. She had a little titter in place of a laugh and she sneezed like a kitten. She always wore high-heels—even around the house—so you'd hear the little pitter-patter of her heels on the parquet floors. After I'd lived in the house for a while, I told Jermaine that we should do a TV sitcom about the place with LaToya in the lead role. In spite of her pretentions, or maybe because of them, she could be riotously funny. It was probably unintentional more often than not. LaToya was like the funny man to Janet's straight man. Janet used to roll her eyes whenever she thought LaToya was acting like a dingbat.

One day LaToya was puttering around the house in her high-heels. As she walked across the recently waxed dining room floor, her feet went out from under her and she landed on her bum. It was one of those situations where you know you shouldn't laugh, and I tried not to, but LaToya was sitting there with this I-just-decided-to-sit-down look on her face.

Janet told me about another time when she and LaToya were out by the pool. LaToya was fooling around on the diving board. Janet warned her not to fall in because she's not a strong swimmer, but of course she did. Katherine, who didn't know how to swim, tried to fish her out with the pool net, with no success. Finally Janet had to jump in, fully clothed, and pull her out.

In another incident, according to Katherine, Janet and LaToya were presenters at an award show. They were backstage and LaToya was fussing with her hair and makeup when Janet told her that if she didn't hurry up they were going to miss their cue. Janet grabbed LaToya's arm and tried to lead her, but LaToya's heels were so high she couldn't run. She stumbled and slipped and finally came onstage looking like she was trying to slide into second base.

The first time I saw LaToya, I was moving into the house and she was descending the grand staircase clad in the tightest pair of white jeans I had ever seen. She was also wearing a teeny little top, a sailor hat, and one huge earring.

Although LaToya almost never ate, when she did her food of choice was air-popped popcorn. On a really special day, she'd have a box of Good & Plenty as well. Like Michael, she got the sweets from the Candy Room, which was accessible by a brick walkway outside of the house. Michael had had the room built, complete with a soda fountain, and filled it with every type of candy imaginable.

Next to the Candy Room was a state-of-the-art recording studio, where Michael recorded much of his *Thriller* album. The house also had its own movie theater with thirty-two plush, red velvet seats and a private projectionist on call day and night. There was also a game room filled with games that Michael would continually update.

Outside there was a miniature zoo and several black and white swans in the man-made pond on the property. The llamas were named Louis and Lola Falana the Llama. The two reindeer were Prince and Princess. And there was a boa constrictor named Rosey. They all looked as if they either stepped or slithered right out of a Walt Disney cartoon. At one point the zoo also had a giraffe named Jabbar, but the neighbors complained that it was always eating the tops off their trees. Michael was forced to give the giraffe away for awhile, and he wasn't very happy about it.

Then there was Bubbles the chimp. When Bubbles wasn't with his trainer, he would live with Michael in his room dressed in diapers and clothing, just like a little kid. Once a new nanny went into the laundry room looking for a clean outfit for my son and mistakenly dressed him in one of Bubbles's costumes, all of which Michael had custom-made.

LaToya was the first family member to welcome me into the fold. In those days she was funny and charming, and smart in her own way. LaToya could act like a fruitcake, but she had a good heart. She seemed innocent and naive. Because I had lived on my own in New York, she would ask me questions about life in the "real world." LaToya was fascinated by actress-model Brigitte Nielsen, who was married to Sylvester Stallone at the time. She wanted to know what I thought about getting a boob job, and about posing for *Playboy* magazine. It was an odd mix of questions that made sense only in retrospect.

Innocent she might have been, but LaToya was a master at getting what she wanted. If she wanted to go shopping, rather than let her drive on her own, Katherine would offer to drive her and give her as much money as she needed. Her mother would drop LaToya off, and if she couldn't find a parking place, she would circle the block until LaToya was finished and ready to go home.

I thought this was amazing. The mother of one of the most famous families on Earth was continually pressed into service as her daughter's chauffeur. LaToya could have driven herself or gotten a ride from someone else in the family, but that was not the way it worked.

LaToya was also a germ fanatic. If you sneezed in her room, she'd immediately spray it with disinfectant. When she left her room she would vacuum the carpet as she backed out. That way, anyone who entered her room while she was gone would leave tell-tale footprints in the carpet.

Jack Gordon, her future husband, had been introduced to the family by Joseph to help LaToya's career. With his pasty skin and scraggly hair, I thought he wasn't much to look at. No matter how much he spent on his suits, nothing seemed to hang properly on his small frame. He seemed an odd choice to help LaToya into the big time, but Joseph hung out with some shady characters and Jack Gordon fit that mold well.

I had been living in the house for only about three weeks when LaToya came charging into our room, obviously agitated. "Quick, Margaret, you've got to do something," she said. "Run downstairs and stop Jack Gordon. He's on his way in here and Joseph's going to start a fight."

LaToya seemed convinced that something awful was going to happen, so I went downstairs. Jack had already entered the house. He was met by Joseph, who took him upstairs to the den, with Katherine bringing up the rear. The den had a comfortable green couch, a TV, and shelves filled with Katherine's collection of books, mainly on black history.

LaToya had been right; it didn't take long for the fighting to start. I walked past the den to get back to my room and heard Joseph berating Jack, calling him a fool. When I entered my room, LaToya was sitting on the hearth of the fireplace. She was crying.

"You don't know this family, Margaret," she sobbed. "My mother is behind all of this. You think she's just the sweetest woman, but she's the one who's pushing Joseph's buttons."

I didn't know what to make of this outburst, since everyone I'd met in the family, up to then, had seemed nice. LaToya continued talking about her mother, the same mother who drove her wherever she wanted to go and gave her whatever she wanted.

"Janet has experienced so many things that I've missed," LaToya said. "Janet's done everything and they won't let me do anything."

She told me about going to some sort of beauty pageant she had hosted in Japan. Katherine and Joseph had also gone as her chaperones. She said they didn't even come to the pageant, opting to stay in their hotel room.

Suddenly she was interrupted by screams coming from the den. Someone was shouting, "Stop it, Joe, you're hurting him!" It was Katherine's voice. Then Katherine started screaming for help. LaToya raced out of my room and down the hallway toward the den. I saw her look inside and start yelling. Joseph evidently was not behaving well.

I was trying to decide if I should try to help or stay out of it when LaToya came rushing back into my room and told me that Joseph had Jack on his knees and was choking him. LaToya began ranting on about Jack's heart condition while I tried to calm her down. Then all was quiet. The fight seemed to have ended as quickly as it had begun.

Later that afternoon LaToya revealed to me that Joseph was angry that Jack had assumed so much control over her career, which was never Joseph's intention. He had brought Jack into the picture to be a babysitter, not the boss. LaToya sided completely with Jack. In her eyes he could do no wrong. I never understood the attraction LaToya had to that man. She was a beautiful, bright, articulate, funny woman from a substantial family in the music industry. What was she doing with him? As far as having sex with Jack, no one will ever convince me she did or would. It's too unthinkable.

As she talked about her father, LaToya started crying again. I felt uncomfortable hearing about her personal affairs, but she seemed to have no reluctance in talking to me even though I was practically a stranger. LaToya said she had spent months on the road with her father, performing with two other girls. "Whichever one he was sleeping with is the one who got the best treatment, got the best room, and sang the leads," she said unhappily. "I don't get it. I'm his daughter." There was sadness in her eyes.

The same bitterness extended to her mother, whom LaToya thought neglected her. She complained that her mother felt she had no talent and was the daughter who would always live at home. "I told her about the way Joseph treated me on the road, how he slept with those girls and how it made me feel. Mother would always say she would do something. She never did," LaToya told me.

LaToya had a lot of tales. She believed her mother had once tried to kill her.

According to LaToya, she went to Katherine and asked for some diuretics before a photo shoot, despite the fact that LaToya's doctor had advised her not to take diuretics. Katherine provided them. Depleted of potassium, LaToya's body was racked by severe muscle spasms, paralyzing her. She screamed out for Katherine, who rushed to LaToya's side, only to reprimand her for taking the drugs she had given her in the first place. In LaToya's mind that constituted intent to commit murder. When I asked Katherine about it, she dismissed LaToya's suspicions as ridiculous.

The day after the fight between Jack Gordon and Joseph, LaToya and Jack were scheduled to fly to New York. Jermaine and I gave them a ride to the airport. LaToya was dressed in a white mink coat and matching hat and carrying two Louis Vuitton bags. At the airport, she got out of the car, turned, and waved good-bye, pausing just a moment longer than usual. As we later realized, she had locked her bedroom door for the last time. As far as I know, she never returned to Hayvenhurst.

With Jack Gordon firmly in control of her career, LaToya moved into a suite at New York City's Waldorf-Astoria Hotel, a changed woman. She launched into a solo career and was booked to perform at Donald Trump's Taj Mahal in Atlantic City.

Jack Gordon phoned Hayvenhurst with the news and spoke with me about the possibility of Jermaine performing a number with his sister. Jack promised to send the Trump plane for us and any other members of the Jackson family who wanted to attend. "LaToya says you're like a sister to her," Jack told me over the phone, trying to enlist my support.

Jermaine wanted no part of the deal and refused to perform with LaToya as long as Jack remained her manager. Eventually Katherine and sisters Rebbie and Janet flew to New York City to see LaToya sing and were amazed at what they found. Visiting LaToya backstage before her appearance, they were startled by the abrupt, unkind way Jack spoke to her. Rebbie and Janet begged her to return home. LaToya's answer was a firm no, along with a denial that Jack was mistreating her in any way.

When we first heard the rumors that LaToya had posed nude for *Playboy* magazine, it was the subject du jour for a while. The idea, of course, put the Jacksons into shock. LaToya was still the little girl who could do no wrong in her mother's eyes. Katherine tracked down LaToya in New York City and begged her to say there was no truth to the story. LaToya responded by claiming she hadn't posed for a Playboy centerfold. It turned out she was right—to a point. The layout of LaToya, which appeared in *Playboy* only weeks later, featured eleven totally nude photographs, including one in which a boa constrictor lounged between her legs. None of her pictures made the centerfold, however. I found the issue at a newsstand near the house and came racing home with it.

"Don't bring that magazine in the house. I don't ever want to see it," Katherine said. "That isn't my daughter." She held up her hands to shield her eyes from the magazine cover.

I went to my room to show the layout to Jermaine. He, too, was annoyed, although I noticed he had no problem examining the photographs up close. In his own fashion, he latched onto LaToya's fifteen minutes of fame by agreeing to do an interview on "Entertainment Tonight," assuming the position of family spokesman. He told the national audience he was embarrassed and humiliated, and mentioned all the impressionable nieces in the Jackson family. Jermaine laid the blame for the photo layout squarely on the shoulders of Jack Gordon, claiming that Jack had manipulated his sister into doing it. Later that day Jermaine called LaToya and was somewhat less polite.

"You little piece of shit!" he shouted. "You've degraded the family and made us all look bad." If LaToya cared, she didn't let on. We didn't know it then, but she was writing a book that would embarrass the family far more than her nude photos did.

At this point Joseph was spending most of his time in Las Vegas, living in a house Katherine had bought there. Michael was off doing his *Bad* tour, which would eventually net him $35 million in cash. Jermaine, Jeremy, and I had the run of the house.

Even though LaToya hadn't turned out to be the big sister I had hoped for, Katherine Jackson seemed to me to be the perfect mother. She would always make time for her children, sometimes listening to them rattle on until all hours of the night as Katherine nodded off in her seat or on the edge of her bed. I always loved it when Janet would come over in the evening and everyone would gather to play Pictionary in the upstairs den. It made me feel like one of the family. After a few months Hayvenhurst finally had begun to feel like home.

Around the same time, Michael had secretly purchased the 2,700-acre Sycamore Ranch in Santa Ynez, California, and renamed it Neverland. Even though I think Katherine knew he was going to do it, the rest of the family heard about it on television and were hurt that Michael hadn't informed them personally. Rumor has it that Michael paid in excess of $35 million for the property. In reality, it cost him just over $17 million, which he paid in cash.

Michael had first stayed at the ranch a few years earlier as a guest of Paul and Linda McCartney while they were renting it. He'd shot the video for the song "Say, Say, Say" at the property with Paul and LaToya. During that visit Paul told Michael how much money could be made in music publishing, information he may later have regretted passing along, because in 1985 Michael bought the entire Beatles library plus the rest of ATV Music Publishing for more than $41 million. The money Michael would soon be making from the Beatles hits could have easily financed the purchase for Neverland.

Michael always told his mother that he would

never leave home until he could purchase the house of his dreams five times over. When he bought Neverland, he had that and more. He wanted to make sure that after he left Hayvenhurst, he never had to come back.

Katherine was sad about him leaving and always hoped he would move back to Hayvenhurst. She didn't even have a chance to speak to Michael as he was moving out because his personal maid, Blanca Francia (whom we called Bianca), removed most of his clothes and books from his room and took them to Neverland. Bianca was a caring, giving person who came from El Salvador with her own son, who would play at the house with Jeremy. I missed them.

A few weeks after we heard about the purchase, Michael invited Katherine, Jermaine, Jeremy, and me down to the ranch for lunch and a tour of the place. We were picked up in a private helicopter at Van Nuys Airport and flown directly to Neverland. Missing from the guest list was Joseph. I questioned Katherine about why he wasn't joining us. "Because that's the way Michael wants it," Katherine replied.

At Neverland I still was curious about Joseph's absence and pushed Katherine into saying something to Michael. We were standing in the kitchen watching Michael peel a pomegranate when Katherine broached the issue.

"Mother, you know I don't want Joseph here, and you know why," Michael said. It was my first clue that things were not right between father and son. The reasons for the hostility between the two would become clearer to me later, but at the time I began to wonder if Katherine didn't enjoy the fact that Joseph was deliberately excluded from so many events and decisions, because it put her in a position of power over him.

In addition to his other dubious qualities, everyone in the family seemed to think Joseph wasn't much of a businessman. He was always getting involved in some kind of deal that turned into a disaster. One such deal blew up in mid-1988.

For years Katherine and Joseph had been involved with a real estate developer named Gary Berwin in a joint venture to build an entertainment complex in L.A. As with almost every venture that Joseph touched, this one was going nowhere. Berwin eventually ran out of patience and sued Joseph, who was ordered to pay Berwin $3 million. Berwin never got the money and must have gotten frustrated waiting. He took out an ad in the *Hollywood Reporter* trying to sell the judgment to the highest bidder. No word on how he made out. Either Michael or Janet could have loaned or given Joseph the money, but bailing

Joseph out of financial trouble had become a habit they'd both given up.

It was at about this time that the Jacksons found a new pot of gold under a different rainbow. This one belonged to the Reverend Sun Myung Moon's Unification Church. The Moonies, for short. A man named Kenneth Choi, a representative of the church, appeared on the scene and began spending time at the Hayvenhurst house. At one point he, his wife, Mirae, and their baby, Elbert, even moved in for a week. Choi offered the family $15 million to perform four concerts in Korea.

Joseph immediately accepted the offer for the entire family, despite the fact that he no longer represented any of them. He got a black Rolls-Royce Corniche for making the deal. Katherine was offered a million in cash if she could guarantee that Michael would perform with the brothers. To her credit, she refused the cash, but did put pressure on her most famous son to bail them out once again.

Jermaine and I went with Rebbie, Katherine, and Randy to Korea for what was supposed to be a meeting with Reverend Moon. He never did see us, but as we sat waiting in the lobby outside his office for an hour, his emissaries kept running in and out.

"Jackson family will help unite Korea," they told us eagerly. "North and South, bring together. Bring together Jackson family, too." We just sat and looked at one another. We didn't know anything about uniting Korea. We were just hanging out.

Money was flowing like water. Choi bought Hazel a new Range Rover. He also bought Jermaine a cream-colored Bentley, which Jermaine drove to Neverland and offered to Michael in the form of a polite bribe. It didn't work. Michael wasn't interested in doing a concert with his brothers. He had already agreed to go to Korea to do a concert for International Children's Day, and his brothers were becoming a stumbling block for that deal.

As things heated up and allegations issued back and forth, news of the scandal started to appear in the tabloids. It was only weeks later that Michael's longtime manager Frank Dileo became victim number one of the new Korean War. Midway during the Moonie mess, Frank was fired in typical Jackson fashion—by telephone from an attorney (in this case John Branca, who would later face the same fate).

With LaToya and Michael both out of the house, Katherine and I seemed to be becoming the best of friends. We would sit on the chairs in the upstairs landing and she would talk about her faith as a Jehovah's Witness. I was fascinated by her struggle to square her religion with what she saw going on in her own house, particularly with Joseph. She was very open about his affairs.

The saddest story was about a woman named Cheryl Terrell. In 1974 Joseph invited Cheryl, who was then in her early twenties, to a party he was throwing at Hayvenhurst while Katherine was away. After everyone left, Cheryl spent the night with Joseph in his and Katherine's bed. Cheryl got pregnant and alerted Joseph that she intended to have the baby. Joh' Vonnie Jackson was born on August 30, 1974, the day after Michael's sixteenth birthday.

Although Joseph placed his name on the birth certificate as Joh' Vonnie's father, he tried to cover his tracks to keep Katherine from discovering what was going on. It took her only a matter of days to learn that there was a new baby girl in the Jackson family, because Joseph's friends continually kept her abreast of her husband's infidelities.

In the past Katherine had always turned a blind eye to Joseph's escapades, but this time would be different. Her first move was to tell each of her children to have absolutely no contact with the mother or child.

"If you see her or have contact with her, you are making what your father did okay, and it is not okay," Katherine had said firmly, adding, "I will never accept that girl into this family." And she never has.

Katherine made it plain that any move toward welcoming the child as a Jackson would be painful for her, and most of her children respected their mother's decision. Her oldest daughter, Rebbie, did not.

As a devoted Jehovah's Witness, Rebbie felt badly for the child and uncomfortable about her mother's attitude. She thought it was only right to check up on Joh' Vonnie periodically and a close relationship began to develop between her and the child. Rebbie would call Jermaine and Janet to come visit Joh' Vonnie when she invited the girl to her home. Both of them went. While Jermaine never extended himself, I think Janet liked the girl and might have made every effort to stay in touch. Unfortunately the Jackson pipeline was totally operational and Katherine discovered what was going on behind her back.

She confronted Janet, who admitted she had met Joh' Vonnie. Janet even made an attempt to get Katherine to see Joseph's daughter. Katherine was not about to be persuaded and told Janet never to see the girl again. The next time Rebbie called Janet to come for a visit, Janet said, "I'm sorry, but if it hurts Mother, I can't come."

Rebbie was not about to be dissuaded. Despite the fact that Katherine issued her the same warning, she continued to encourage Joh' Vonnie's friendship. One afternoon, while Katherine was out of town, Rebbie called and said she was bringing Joh' Vonnie over to Hayvenhurst for a grand tour. Joseph was home at the time and took his daughter into every room, including his own, allowing her to sit on his bed. When I saw Joh' Vonnie in their bedroom, I could only imagine what would have happened if Katherine had walked through the door.

In the end, Katherine never did find out about Joh' Vonnie's visit. I could have told her, but I didn't want to cause problems. I didn't want to hurt her feelings. Little did I know I was inadvertently about to do just that.

5

I'm pregnant," I told Katherine after receiving confirmation. She broke into a smile that would have reached from Encino all the way back to Gary, Indiana, and we started jabbering away the way expectant moms and grandmothers do.

I first realized a second child might be on the way in mid-1988 when I agreed to do a photo shoot with Jermaine for the back cover of his *Two Ships* album. I kept trying on different outfits. Nothing fit. The stylist who was helping us gave me a knowing look, but I didn't catch on. Finally Jermaine asked me if I thought I might be pregnant. After the photo shoot I had tests done and received the word.

As soon as I heard the news, I ran to tell

Katherine, eager for her blessing. I later found out she was happy partially because she thought Jermaine and I would finally set a wedding date. She loved the fact that we were living in the house but wanted our relationship legalized. She thought my pregnancy would ensure that we would take that step.

In my own happiness I wasn't thinking about anything except my new baby and making the necessary preparations. I asked Katherine if she thought we could have more room. It was a loaded question, but Jermaine, Jeremy, and I had been living in one room and I knew it would be impossible to put another baby into that space. I saw Katherine struggling with the answer: Although both Michael and LaToya's rooms were empty, Katherine kept hoping they would both move back home someday.

There was a guest room downstairs, but that was too far from the room Jermaine and I shared with Jeremy. When I told her it might be best if we got our own place, her face fell. Still, there was no way she was going to give us Michael or LaToya's room.

Word of my condition spread throughout the household and everyone seemed genuinely excited about the news, Jeremy included. More than anything, Jermaine hoped our next child would be a girl. He had said he wanted a daughter during my first pregnancy, and when Jeremy was born, I knew he loved his son even though he was a little disappointed. This would be my second chance to give him a baby girl.

Every time he brought up the subject of having a daughter, I couldn't help but remember Dawn. The mysterious Dawn. Her name first came up while Jermaine and I were living in our condo in Pacific Palisades. He mentioned he knew this girl named Dawn who lived in Atlanta, Georgia. He said that she had been abandoned by her father and that he had grown close to her, even providing financial assistance when her mother asked. I tried to be accepting because I knew Hazel had allowed this girl's visits and had put up with Dawn for entire summers. Putting aside my reservations, I invited her to visit for a few weeks.

When I first met Dawn in 1987 she was about eleven years old, a tall, pretty, light-skinned girl with a nice personality and one annoying habit: She called Jermaine "Daddy." I was embarrassed and upset that he would allow it. When I asked him for an explanation, Jermaine said it was nothing. He told me Dawn had been calling him Daddy since the day they met. She followed Jermaine around like a puppy dog and looked up to him with unbridled adulation. He could do no wrong in this girl's eyes. It was always "Daddy" this, "Daddy" that, from the time she arrived until the time she left. The entire relationship puzzled and bothered me.

As sweet as she was, I was always relieved when she left. Having her gone, however, didn't stop her influence on our lives. Her mother would call on the phone asking for money and Jermaine would always try to scrape some cash together. I always wondered why. Whenever we moved, Dawn would follow us from house to house, eventually visiting us at Hayvenhurst soon after I discovered I was pregnant again. Katherine was as perplexed as I was.

"Margaret, I don't understand. Where did this girl come from?" she asked. The best I could do was shrug my shoulders, relieved in my heart that Katherine didn't look upon her as another grandchild. By this time the girl was about five feet six inches tall and was still sitting on Jermaine's lap, calling him Daddy. It was enough to wear anyone's patience thin.

In the meantime I had ballooned with pregnancy number two and had to watch this thin young thing hang all over Jermaine. It was embarrassing and pathetic. The only one who failed to understand how inappropriate it was was Jermaine.

Dawn went with us when we took a trip to New Jersey to visit Eddie Murphy at his estate, Bubble Hill. What I remember most about that trip was feeling uncomfortable. No, make that miserable. There I was in the back seat of the limo—187 pounds, my stomach out to *there*—squashed between Dawn, Jermaine, his brother Jackie, and Wallace Farrakhan, the son of Nation of Islam leader Louis Farrakhan. I recall sitting in Eddie's house watching a group of tall, thin, beautiful young models run around in skin-tight dresses. At dinner Dawn took every opportunity to address Jermaine as Daddy.

Later that night, back in our hotel room, I lost it. I told Jermaine the time had come to put a stop to the humiliation. I said I didn't care how often she visited, I didn't care if he wanted to send her money, but there was no way I was going to stand for this virtual stranger continually calling him Daddy. At that point Dawn came in. She walked over to Jermaine and put her arms around him. He looked at me and said, "No one else knows, Margaret, but Dawn really *is* my daughter. I had an affair with her mother years ago."

I didn't know whether to cry or burst out laughing. I told him that I didn't believe him; that she didn't even look like him. Dawn said,

"Well, what's the difference, anyway? It all happened before he knew you."

I was so angry I called Katherine in California. I needed someone with some common sense to talk to. I deserved at least that. I had dealt with a soon-to-be ex-wife, young children, attorneys, managers, LaToya's naked pictures, Joseph's extramarital affairs, and Michael's chimpanzee. But this was too much.

Katherine was, as usual, the voice of reason. "Don't worry about it, Margaret," she told me. "There's no way that girl could be Jermaine's daughter without my knowledge. Forget it. It'll blow over."

She was right. The girl went back to Atlanta and the calls from her mother became less frequent, at least for a while.

Is Dawn actually Jermaine's daughter? I guess I'll never know for sure.

Back at Hayvenhurst, Katherine was increasing the pressure on Michael to perform in Korea. Joseph, wisely, had headed to the house in Las Vegas and was staying out of sight. Jermaine was busy continuing to record 2300 *Jackson Street* when, in August 1988, an article in *People* magazine told the world about my pregnancy. Jermaine brought the magazine home to show to Jermaine Jr. and Autumn, who had come to

Hayvenhurst for a visit. At the end of the day, their father put them in the car and left to return them to Hazel. By this time she was living in a large house her father had gotten for her.

That evening Jermaine and I had planned on going out to dinner with my stepfather, Cy. I was excited about seeing him again. After a while, though, I became nervous because Jermaine was late in getting back home.

Then the telephone rang. It was Hazel.

"Jermaine was just here, and he tried to rape me," she said, her voice shaking.

"What?" was all I could say. I was unwilling and unable to grasp what I was hearing.

"I'm not lying, Margaret. People who know me know that I do not lie. And if you don't believe me, look at Jermaine's arm. I bit it," she added.

After a long pause I told Hazel that if what she was saying was true, she should call the police and report it. She did just that.

I didn't want to believe Hazel. I didn't want to believe that Jermaine could attempt to rape his former wife, then go out to dinner with my stepfather and me as if nothing had happened.

When Jermaine pulled into the driveway, I didn't know what to expect. I told him about Hazel's call as calmly as possible. Jermaine denied it. He said Hazel was jealous because she had read about my pregnancy and just wanted to upset me. I looked at Jermaine's arm and his clothes. I could see no bite mark or any other signs of a struggle. Still, Hazel was so convincing on the phone that I wasn't completely buying his denial. One of them was lying and I didn't know whom.

Totally stressed out, I rushed from the house, got in my car, and drove around for several hours trying to think what to do next. When I returned to Hayvenhurst, I was relieved to see no police cars. I began hoping that perhaps the incident had blown over. What I didn't expect was to find Katherine waiting up for me. She sat me down and said she wanted to give me some advice. "If you want a relationship to work, you can't run off like that, Margaret. You stay and you finish it. Work things out."

She made perfect sense. I nodded in agreement. She took the time to reassure me that she had talked with Jermaine and believed her son when he said he hadn't done what Hazel said.

Unfortunately, the charges didn't go away that easily. A couple of days later, the police did show up at Hayvenhurst and took a statement from Jermaine. I was emotionally exhausted by the whole thing and hoped it would go away.

When the divorce became final in November,

I expected that Jermaine and I would get married. I waited for him to bring up the subject and half expected a surprise engagement ring. It never happened. When I broached the issue, he told me to be patient. He was busy trying to finalize the settlement with Hazel over their property and child support, he said.

As things turned out, it was a lucky break. After the alleged rape attempt, Hazel began to play hardball and demanded a steady flow of money. Despite Jermaine's constant assurances that she would get the money when he did, it was never enough.

She served both Jermaine and me with subpoenas requiring us to give depositions regarding Jermaine's bank accounts and business dealings. Hazel wanted to know the specific details of his record deal, how much money he was spending on me, and how much he had in liquid assets. She demanded information about car payments, rent, clothing allowances, charge cards, the works. In hindsight, it's easy for me to understand Hazel's frustration. To the world, Jermaine Jackson was a rich man. In private, however, he was being hounded by creditors and owed an enormous amount in taxes. Jermaine was growing more and more content to live off of his brother Michael. He didn't ask for money, but Michael paid all the Hayvenhurst bills.

At one point Jermaine's debt had grown so large that I sat down with his business manager, Howard Grossman, and we had a serious discussion about Jermaine filing for Chapter 11 protection. During the course of a later meeting at the office of Bill Glucksman, the attorney who was handling Jermaine's divorce settlement, Bill suggested to Jermaine that they pursue the idea of making a declaration of bankruptcy. To Jermaine, who had already agreed to make a $200,000 settlement to Hazel, the sound of bankruptcy was music to his ears.

Then Bill insisted that all of us listen to what Hazel had declared in her police report. Jermaine tried to dissuade him, and I backed him up, but Bill held firm. By this time I was eight months pregnant and didn't need to get upset over this particular issue again. He read it anyway.

According to Hazel, while Jermaine was driving the kids home that day, he told them that he wanted to have another baby with their mother. He told the kids that when they got home, they should go to their rooms so he could speak to Hazel about it. If they heard any shouting, he said, they should just ignore it. It would only be Mom and Dad playing. When Jermaine found Hazel, he threw her on the bed, pushed up her skirt, and tried to rip off her underwear. Hazel screamed for Jermaine Jr. and Autumn, but neither of them came.

After Bill read the deposition, Jermaine was outraged. The attorney was embarrassed. I was sick. I couldn't understand how Hazel could be so graphic and involve her children if, as Jermaine said, there was no truth to the story. As a mother, I couldn't believe any woman would do that simply out of spite. I knew Hazel had been telling the truth—if not the whole truth, at least a good part of it. In the end the charges against Jermaine were thrown out on a technicality. Jermaine never brought up the issue again, nor did he ever declare bankruptcy.

The bankruptcy discussions, however, did prove fateful as far as any marriage plans were concerned. Grossman advised me against marrying him at that point because of his enormous tax liability. Since Jermaine was about to go on tour again, it was suggested that he route his income through me. The matter was handled by setting up a corporation called Margaret's Tours Inc., and naming me as president. I suddenly found myself the conduit for all of Jermaine's funds.

Jermaine was not the only one in the family with money problems, but his were the most pressing. Tito and his wife, DeeDee, at least still had their home in Encino. Marlon and Carol had their home near Tito's house. Jackie and Enid had divorced and Enid had gotten the $200,000 settlement. Jackie had moved into a condo. Randy was still in his condo on Wilshire and riding around on his Harley-Davidson motorcycle.

The brothers' problem wasn't one of current cash flow, but rather future cash flow. More was going out than was coming in. Each of their solo albums went nowhere, and ultimately that was the same place the last Jackson album, 2300 *Jackson Street,* was headed.

Without Michael's or Janet's help, I knew the others were going to need a new source of revenue soon. It was then that the idea of the miniseries came to me.

As my pregnancy stretched into full-term, I began spending more and more of my time just sitting and talking with Katherine. She would tell me about the early days of the Jacksons, before they made it into the big time. I thought the stories were unique and special. Our favorite spot to chat continued to be the two chairs on the upstairs landing, and it was there, during a conversation, that I first mentioned to her the idea of doing a television show about the family and how the Jacksons came to be. At that point I didn't know how to go about making it a reality. What I *did* know was that musical biographies were big on TV. I had just finished watching two different versions of the Liberace story as well as the film bio of Karen Carpenter. Why not the Jackson family?

Katherine laughed when I told her about my idea of turning them into a TV movie, saying no one would be interested in watching a story about her family. "I wouldn't ever watch a movie about the Osmonds," she added.

I tried to explain to her how important the Jacksons' story could be to young people, particularly young black people. I explained that television rarely does a positive black drama and that whenever it does it's only if the black person is dead. I also said the movie would be a good vehicle for all the fine black actors out there. "Everybody could have input and it could turn out to be a wonderful family project," I stressed, knowing full well how much that could mean to Katherine. She thought about it for a while, then smiled and nodded. That was enough for me.

I talked to Jermaine and outlined my idea to him. I sweetened it for him by telling him he could produce the show and open up an entirely new direction in his career. Jermaine agreed to bring it up at a meeting he was having with his agent, Brian Gersh, at the Triad Agency. Brian's eyes lit up as he thought about putting the Jackson family saga on television and his enthusiasm for the project was reinforced by another agent, Rob Lee, who began to lay the groundwork.

"Only if Jermaine produces," I emphasized.

"No problem. No problem at all," Rob agreed. He was all smiles at the prospect of getting Jermaine some income. Rob's only reservation was the uncertainty about getting Michael to agree to the project. Michael's participation would be the key. By this time everyone in town knew that Michael had severed his professional ties with the family and was living at his Neverland Ranch in Santa Ynez. I told Rob that Michael respects people who are accomplished and always likes to deal with top persons in the field. "Find the best executive producer in the business, and Michael will join our team just to learn from him. He's like a sponge," I said.

Rob Lee suggested we make an offer to one of his clients, Stan Margulies, a legend in Hollywood. He had produced *The Thorn Birds* as well as the multipart *Moviola*, about the early days of film. His features included *Willy Wonka and the Chocolate Factory*. His biggest credit was for *Roots*, perhaps the best miniseries ever.

Stan came over to Hayvenhurst and had lunch

with Katherine, Jermaine, and me. He charmed all of us. He was soft-spoken, almost scholarly, and seemed to have invested a lot of himself in every production he undertook. He was invited to join the team and accepted. Everyone was pleased.

Next came Suzanne de Passe. As an early employee of Berry Gordy at Motown, Suzanne had discovered the Jackson 5 and had been involved with them in a number of ways from the beginning. She had since become a major player in the Hollywood community, having been nominated for an Academy Award for cowriting the screenplay for *Lady Sings the Blues*. She had also served as executive producer of the Emmy Award-winning "Motown 25," Michael's 1988 TV special, and the megahit miniseries *Lonesome Dove*, among others. I was excited about meeting and working with her.

Suzanne was even more wonderful than I could have anticipated. When we met with her, not only did she want to participate, but she also offered to help gain Berry Gordy's cooperation as well. Since Berry still controlled all the music rights to the early Jackson hits, his involvement would be essential.

I had asked Katherine to keep Joseph away from this project. I said this could be one thing that could actually produce real money for the family for the future. She saw my point. To protect ourselves, I suggested to Katherine that we form a company called KJ Films Inc. and funnel all the money through it. KJ Films would do the hiring, handle the writing of checks, and act as a central clearinghouse for the miniseries. Joseph was not involved in any way.

Because the project was owned by Katherine and me, we were concerned about creditors trying to collect the debts of individual Jackson family members. To head off any lawsuits and liens, I was voted 50 percent of stock in KJ Films; Katherine held the remaining 50 percent. I was chairman of the board, chief executive officer, and secretary. Katherine was president, chief financial officer, and treasurer.

As the project began to take shape, my involvement on Jermaine's behalf grew so much that one of our attorneys suggested that I speak to Jermaine about sharing credit on the miniseries since I was doing most of the work. I hadn't thought about sharing the producing credit at all. All I was certain I could produce was babies. And I was very uncomfortable about going to Jermaine and asking for anything. As it turned out, I didn't have to. The attorneys did it for me.

Jermaine agreed that I was doing a great job,

and agreed to share credit. I was thrilled. Not only was I being recognized for a job performance for the first time in my life, I was being given the opportunity to open a career door for Jermaine. And for myself.

I jumped at the chance and sprinted through that open door with enthusiasm. Unfortunately, when I looked back, Jermaine hadn't come through the door with me.

6

On January 5, 1989, Jourdynn Michael Jackson was born. Considering what I had gone through with the birth of Jeremy, Jourdynn's arrival was a vacation. I was in the hospital for a total of four hours.

I decided there would be no repeat performances of me rushing to Cedars-Sinai only to be sent home. This time, when I started into labor, Jermaine and I went to a pharmacy, and by the time I was done buying an extra toothbrush and toothpaste, I told Jermaine we should go.

Jermaine took me to the hospital and they kept me. In fact, I was so far along into the birth process that the doctor said he couldn't give me the drugs I had taken during my previous pregnancy. The idea of natural childbirth was about as appealing to me as a root canal without anesthesia. I began unhooking myself from all the monitors and equipment and announced I was leaving for someplace that had *major* drugs.

Jermaine got on the phone and quickly received a doctor's approval for a sedative. I was immediately rolled into the delivery room and two hours later, there was Jourdynn. Jermaine and I had already decided on his name but had not discussed the spelling. By the time I was out of the recovery room, Jermaine had filled out the birth certificate and our new son had a few extra letters in his name. When we returned to the Hayvenhurst house that evening, Jourdynn was placed in the upstairs den. My new nanny, Heidi, was going to have to sleep on the sofa. It wasn't an ideal solution to our housing problems, but one we all would have to tolerate for the time being.

During the next few weeks, all of the family members except LaToya came to see little Jourdynn. Michael would drive in from Neverland unannounced, come into the den late at night, and just stand there looking at Jourdynn in his bassinet. Several minutes later he would leave as quietly as he had arrived.

Because the Korean family tour was still in negotiation, both Joseph and Kenneth Choi were spending a lot of time at Hayvenhurst. I'd wake up and Choi was there. I'd go to sleep and Choi was there. Joseph's business manager, Jerome Howard, was ever-present as well, working overtime to keep the Korean deal from going up in smoke.

That was a minor distraction compared to the constant infighting that was taking place between the brothers. Not a day went by that one or more of them wouldn't be on the phone in an uproar. Jackie, Tito, Randy, and Jermaine were still recording *2300 Jackson Street* and it was the cause of constant consternation between them. Jermaine complained about Tito spending too much time with his cars and model airplanes. The buzz on Randy was that he was never around when they needed him. They nicknamed him "Grand Opening" because they said all he had time for was the opening of a new restaurant or nightclub.

But nothing was as bad as the back-and-forth bickering between Jermaine and Jackie. Both of them wanted to sing the lead vocals on every song on the album. Jermaine was in the studio during the day singing the leads with Jackie and sometimes Tito as backup. At night Jackie rerecorded the same song singing the lead vocals himself. The next day, when the tape arrived at

Hayvenhurst, Jermaine went ballistic. This went on for months.

The recording was not the only topic of discussion. The girlfriend merry-go-round gave them all something to talk about. Jackie, now divorced from Enid and done with Paula Abdul, had begun to see a girl named Victoria. At the same time he was seeing a beautiful actress named Leela Rashawn, whom everyone called Shawnie. She was known as the "Budweiser girl" and appeared in all those commercials with the dog Spuds MacKenzie and later went on to appear in several Eddie Murphy films. One day Victoria would be at the house. The next day it would be Shawnie. Neither of them knew about the other's existence. It got even worse when Jackie and Victoria became officially engaged and Jackie continued to bring Shawnie to the house.

That was mild compared to what was going on with Randy. Randy was seeing a beautiful Persian girl named Eliza Shaffe, whom he'd met at a nightclub. Eliza was also dating Gabriel Horowitz, a professional gambler and former husband of Marcia Clark, lead prosecutor in the O. J. Simpson trial. Randy was crazy about Eliza, but not quite crazy enough that he didn't have another girlfriend on the side. He had met Alijandra Loaiza while she was still attending Beverly

Hills High School. He had escorted her to her graduation and rented an apartment for her soon afterward. That relationship remained hot until the afternoon Randy made a surprise visit to the apartment and found Alijandra in bed with her best friend's boyfriend. Randy was so upset he ran outside and sat crying on the curb. A neighbor brought him a glass of water to calm him down. Alijandra and Randy broke up and he began seriously dating Eliza. Things seemed to settle down after that, but what Randy didn't know was that Alijandra was pregnant with his child.

At first, no one in the family knew about *either* girlfriend. Randy was always out on the town. He did bring Eliza by Hayvenhurst once, and Katherine definitely did *not* like what she saw.

Eliza was a pretty girl who wore too much makeup and often dressed in tight blue jeans and a denim shirt tied under her braless breasts. Not someone you would necessarily want Mother to meet—unless of course, you had married the girl, which, it turned out, Randy had, having eloped with Eliza in August 1990. She was pregnant, too.

I met Alijandra by accident when I happened to be shopping in a Beverly Hills boutique where she worked. I was wearing a Jacksons T-shirt. As

I walked around I was approached by Alijandra, who asked where I'd gotten my top. I told her I was Jermaine's wife, and she pulled me aside and told me her name and said she was pregnant with Randy's baby. *The plot thickens,* I thought. Alijandra had moved out of the apartment Randy had rented for her and was living with her teenage brother. She said she couldn't pay her doctor bills and was barely able to put food on the table.

Sympathizing with her position, I told her I would see if I could get the Jacksons to help her financially, and I promised to give her my old baby furniture, which was in storage. I took this bit of news back to Hayvenhurst, only to find that Randy had married Eliza and she was also carrying his baby.

Randy had been a very busy man.

Amid the ongoing negotiations between Joseph, Kenneth Choi, and Jerome Howard; the pregnant and nonpregnant girlfriends; and the fact that my newborn was living in a den and his nanny was sleeping on a sofa, I knew it was time for us to strike out on our own. Over Katherine's objections, Jermaine and I found a beautiful two-bedroom condo on Burton Way in Beverly Hills for $3,000 a month. At the time we could afford it. I knew there would be money coming in from the miniseries, Jermaine was still doing the occasional concert, and he was continuing to receive between $12,000 and $25,000 a month as part of his advance from Arista Records.

Katherine helped me select furniture for our new home and I was strongly influenced by her taste. We wound up with ornate Italianate furniture in the living room, and a dining room table that looked like something out of "The Addams Family." It had claws on the legs and the chair seats were crushed velvet. In spite of that, I was happy to call the place home. It was also wonderful to have Jermaine to myself for the first time in a year. Our relationship was still good, although there was no talk of marriage in our immediate future. But I was excited about the miniseries, adored my two children, and had a solid relationship. My life was moving along happily. Then came a big bump in the road.

One day Jermaine told me he wanted me to meet some dear friends as we pulled into a driveway on North Rodeo Drive, not far from the Beverly Hills Hotel. The house was fronted by a set of enormous black gates.

"This is Madam Bongo's house," Jermaine informed me. "She threw a big dinner in honor of my family a few years back and I'd like you to meet her." The thought of meeting someone named Madam Bongo was not on my official schedule that day or any other day I could possibly imagine. But, to please Jermaine, I agreed. Madam Bongo, it seemed, was the former wife of Omar Bongo, the president of Gabon, a country in West Africa rich in uranium, magnesium, petroleum, and lumber. Jermaine told me that Madam had divorced President Bongo and now wanted to become a singer, so she had moved to Beverly Hills and had started work on an album.

Of all of Jermaine's friends, this was one of the few whose advance billing was nothing compared to the real thing.

We rang the doorbell and were escorted into the kitchen of an ornate, overdecorated house. Despite the presence of two automatic dishwashers, there were dishes piled everywhere. I was introduced to a short, fat woman who was seated in the middle of the large room, having her hair braided by three young girls. Half of her head was being braided with extensions, while the rest was in short, stubby little spikes. Covering nearly all her face were big, gold-rimmed sunglasses.

That was my introduction to Madam Bongo. She was so rude to me that I thought perhaps she didn't speak English. Jermaine went over and gave her a kiss and introduced me. I barely heard more than a grunt from the woman in my direction. To Jermaine, however, she was warm and open and invited us back that evening for dinner. I was not thrilled. I was deliberately made to feel uncomfortable by this woman and would have been perfectly happy to pass on the invite. It seemed important to Jermaine, though, so that evening I dressed in something appropriately gaudy and arrived back at Madam Bongo's door with Jermaine.

During the meal I was introduced to Madam's half-sister, Lea. Same father, different mother. Lea was a bright, chunky, seventeen-year-old African girl who had gone to a Swiss boarding school and was now studying petroleum engineering and international business at UCLA. Lea was the only one who paid much attention to me. Madam and Jermaine were busy discussing business, including Jermaine's availability to sing on Madam's album. Madam Bongo did not have a record deal but she had more than enough money to finance and produce an album on her own. She had so much money, in fact, that she bought an entire recording studio in Hollywood. As Madam saw it, having Jermaine on the album would put her right over the top.

We ate dinner in the living room, which was decorated with inlaid ivory. Twenty Moroccans had been flown in for the job. Gold-and-white Italian chairs were arranged in a circle on an enormous Persian rug. The meal was served on paper plates by an assortment of little children whom Madam had adopted in Africa and brought to the United States. She was putting the children through school at the Lycée Française. She also had a group of teenage girls to look after them, and Jermaine looked like he was loving the attention of these girls.

After dinner, Madam sang and played the conga. She actually performed an entire show as we sat there, dinner plates on our laps, watching. She was joined in the center of the room by the teenage girls, who performed provocative African dances. Jermaine obviously found the raw movements captivating, so much so that we began to return to Madam's house for dinner nearly every night.

I put a lot of effort into trying to be friendly with the Bongo group. They were loud, rude, boring strangers, but I was determined. Lea continued to be the only one I could have a conversation with and we began to form a friendship that would have its ups and downs for years.

Although there had been a steady flow of money, Jermaine's record company was getting tired of giving him advances and began to worry about recouping their money. Hazel's alimony and child support payments were causing us to reach the bottom of the cash barrel. In mid-1989 things got so tight that Jermaine had to part with his favorite toy—his midnight-blue Ferrari Daytona. Having that car seemed pretentious, so I was not sad to see it go, but Jermaine was heartbroken. It had been his status symbol, his proof of stardom, and now it was no more. Ironically, Hazel had bought him the car as a birthday present when they were married and now he was selling the car to pay Hazel's alimony.

Once the car sold and we got the money, Hazel got $20,000 of it and with the rest we paid overdue bills. I'd asked Jermaine's business managers Ralph Goldman and Howard Grossman if there was some way we might use some of the cash to buy Jermaine a used Rolls-Royce Corniche as a surprise. I might as well have asked them to consider buying Jermaine a bridge over Lake Erie. Then a little luck kicked in. Restaurateur George Santo-Pietro (who later married Vanna White) had bought Jermaine's Ferrari and had a black Corniche for sale. After negotiating a great price, I bought it for Jermaine and had it waiting in the garage for him.

Soon after, we were calling the moving trucks again. Our two boys were growing older and needed some outdoor play room. I found a perfect house off of Beverly Glen Drive in Los Angeles.

When our six-month lease on the Burton Way condo ended, we packed up and headed to our new home. It was less money than the condo and a much bigger place for us all.

At the same time Michael bought a condo on the fourteenth floor of the Westford on Wilshire Boulevard because he was required to be in town on business and wanted a place to stay. His new condominium was a large, modern three-bedroom place that his nephews nicknamed "The Hideout." It was nice but nothing fancy. It was the favorite place of DeeDee and Tito's children, Taj, Terrel, and T.J., to play.

Michael's star was skyrocketing while his brothers were floundering. When 2300 *Jackson Street* was released, sales were so poor that Sony Records dropped the Jacksons' contract. It was a real blow to the brothers, who had spent most of their lives with fame and its rewards, which had come to them so easily. This was a new reality, one that was difficult for them to grasp.

While the rest of the brothers continued to struggle with money, Michael was almost being buried under it. His latest deal—to become the spokesman for L.A. Gear athletic shoes—brought him $20 million for a two-year hitch. Although that contract would eventually result in a lawsuit, it at least generated some positive publicity for the Jackson name. It was a name that was received well, as long as the first name was Michael or Janet. In January 1990 Michael received the American Cinema Award for Entertainer of the Year. In April Janet received a star on Hollywood Boulevard's Walk of Fame. That same month President George Bush labeled Michael "Entertainer of the Decade" on the day that Michael helped Donald Trump open the Taj Mahal Casino in Atlantic City.

There was sadness, too. Weeks after being in Atlantic City, Michael and Donald Trump flew to Indiana in Trump's private jet to attend the funeral of teenager Ryan White, who had died of AIDS. Ryan had been a guest of Michael's at Neverland several times during the course of his illness, and Michael had given the boy a red Mustang convertible for his sixteenth birthday. Ryan White's death had a profound impact on Michael. He increased his private efforts to raise money for AIDS organizations and would put a musical tribute to Ryan—"Gone Too Soon"—on his next album.

I was hard at work on the miniseries and it had begun to take up a healthy chunk of my time. Suzanne de Passe hired a woman named Joyce Eliason to write the screenplay and Joyce was preparing to interview each of the family members about his or her childhood and the early years of the Jackson 5. Joyce had previously written the ABC miniseries *Elvis and Me* which made her an easy sell to Michael, who had writer approval. Joyce had worked before with Suzanne on the ABC miniseries *Small Sacrifices* (a Motown production), and she turned out to be a wonderful working partner.

As the miniseries began to take over my life, I saw Jermaine ease out of the entire project. Not only did he seem to lose interest in it, but he also began to belittle it. "I don't have time for a little miniseries, Margaret," he'd say. "I'm going to build a movie studio in Africa and I'm working on an amusement park in Asbury Park, New Jersey. I don't have time for this."

Jermaine was cooking up these business ventures with a new partner named Bob Petrallia. Bob was an entrepreneur who had worked for Warner Communications and was supposed to be setting Jermaine up in his own business, Jackson Communications Inc. (JCI).

In addition to the supposed plans for a movie studio and amusement park, Bob had convinced Jermaine that they were going to build a recording studio, a Jackson family museum, and a record company named Work Records. When I heard about the grand scale of all these projects, it was all I could do to keep from laughing out loud. Jermaine was not a natural businessman and I thought he was being suckered into some questionable deals. What concerned me was that he did have legitimate business to prepare for. He was about to start recording a new album, this time with new producers and a new label.

When Jermaine's *Two Ships* album came out and the title song reached number one on the R&B charts, Arista Records president Clive Davis decided to assign Jermaine's contract to L.A.Face Records, a joint venture between L.A. (Antonio Reid), BabyFace (Kenny Edmonds), and Arista. By moving to the new label, Jermaine was assured that the hot producers would give Jermaine major attention on his next album.

During this time we heard some frightening news on the television that would temporarily bring all our projects to a halt. On June 3, 1990, word had reached the newsrooms that Michael Jackson had had a heart attack and had been rushed to Saint John's Hospital in Santa Monica. Jermaine immediately called Marlon to see if he had heard anything. Marlon never called back, so Jermaine and I went to the hospital to learn what we could about Michael's condition.

When we arrived at Saint John's, we learned that Michael had gotten chest pains and passed out while he was practicing some dance routines at the Hideout. When he woke up, he called his friend and plastic surgeon, Dr. Steven Hoefflin, who rushed to his side. After detecting an irregular heartbeat, Hoefflin drove Michael immediately to Saint John's.

The hospital floor Michael was on had more security than the White House. You needed a laminated pass just to breathe the air. There were guards at the elevator, guards at the nurses' stations, and uniformed people everywhere, and for good reason. In the room on one side of Michael was Ronald Reagan. On the other side was Elizabeth Taylor.

We went into Michael's room. He was all alone, sitting up in bed wearing a hospital gown and his black fedora. As Jermaine sat down next to the bed to talk with his brother, I peeked into the closet and saw only a little pair of black pants folded up, a red shirt hanging on a hanger, and black shoes on the floor.

Although Michael looked to me as if he was feeling fine, the doctors told him he needed to stay overnight for observation. Noting that there was no robe, underwear, slippers, or anything else a patient in a hospital might need, I left to go shopping for a few things to tide Michael over. At Robinson's I bought Michael a flannel robe, pajamas, leather slippers, and some underwear. When I returned, my gift was received with thanks and an invitation to leave. Elizabeth Taylor was going to visit and Michael wanted some privacy. Jermaine made a wisecrack about Elizabeth and was quickly put in his place. "Don't ever talk bad about Elizabeth Taylor to me, Jermaine," Michael said softly. "She's beautiful. The most beautiful woman I've ever met."

By this time Michael and Elizabeth were already well acquainted, but their friendship would grow during this brief stay in the hospital. She came for visits several times a day and sometimes brought him violets, which stood in sweet contrast to the dozen black roses LaToya had had delivered from London.

During the week Michael was in the hospital, Jermaine slept over in the room one night. Janet came to visit once, having put her *Rhythm Nation 1814* tour on hold to see Michael. Elton John stopped by, as did Liza Minnelli. Only after it was determined that he was suffering from costochondritis, a harmless inflammation of the ribs, was Michael allowed to leave.

Jermaine told Michael about his new contract with L.A. Face Records. He was excited about the prospect of working with L.A. and BabyFace, who would be producing his entire album.

"Mike, these guys could be for me like Jimmy Jam and Terry Lewis were for Janet," Jermaine said enthusiastically. Jimmy Jam Harris and Terry Lewis were the writing-producing team that had turned Janet Jackson's *Control* and *Rhythm Nation 1814* albums into superhits.

Apparently, the fact that Jermaine had scored bigtime with L.A. and BabyFace was not lost on his brother. Only days after getting out of the hospital, Michael began a set of negotiations with the producers that would affect his relationship with Jermaine forever.

7

Plastic surgery. There should be a footnote to this entry in the dictionary that says: *see Jackson Family*. Although the plastic surgery Michael Jackson has had done on his nose and his chin has made headlines all over the world, what hasn't made the news is that nearly all of the members of the family, including Joseph and Katherine, have had various parts of their faces and bodies altered, Jermaine included. Jermaine had his nose operated on for the first time while we still lived in the Hayvenhurst house, but he broke with family tradition and didn't use Dr. Steven Hoefflin, whose work had never impressed him. Instead, Jermaine went to Dr. Raj Kanodia of Beverly Hills.

He went to Dr. Kanodia again when we lived

in our home off Beverly Glen. This go-round, Jermaine wanted an even smaller nose and higher cheeks and Dr. Kanodia obliged. Jermaine came home with bandages wrapped around his face. He looked like something out of *The Mummy's Curse*. Having your nose fixed is one thing, but the thought of cheek implants gave me the willies. I kept imagining Jermaine as an old man with his cheeks slipping down to his chin. He never mentioned to me he was having the surgery done, and probably never would have told me if the bandages hadn't made it so obvious.

I had always thought Jermaine was very good-looking and was amazed that he felt he continually needed to "adjust" certain features. It was an ongoing process, one I never got used to. Picture getting into bed every night with a man with cold cream on his face, his hair in a silk bonnet, and a metal clamp with screws on each side to keep his nose from growing larger. It was an incredible sight.

Jermaine's vanity was tempered by his spontaneous gestures of thoughtfulness. He had often said it was a shame I had never reconnected with my biological father, Bill, who was still living in Oregon. As a surprise for my father's fiftieth birthday, he took me, my brother, and Jeremy and Jourdynn to visit him. I was sure my dad and Jermaine would get along well, and they did.

After we got back, Jermaine started traveling frequently on what he described as business trips. I was busy myself, laying the groundwork for the miniseries and continuing my efforts to bring some of the other wives into the project. Of all the wives, Tito's wife, DeeDee, was my favorite and I urged her to join me on the production. At the time, however, she was having marital problems and, as usual with the Jackson men, it involved infidelity.

On the surface, the marriage of Tito and DeeDee was the most perfect of any of the Jacksons. Tito loved his three sons and was constantly involved in all of their school and sporting events, including teaching their Little League team. DeeDee was the model mother, the one who drove the car pool, attended the PTA meetings, fixed the lunches, and kissed the scrapes to make them better. Her marriage to Tito came crashing down one summer afternoon when DeeDee drove to their home in Oxnard. It was a beautiful place on the water where they kept their boat, a large cabin cruiser. She was planning a surprise visit to Tito who had been spending more and more time at that home and away from DeeDee and the kids at their Encino home.

When she got to the Oxnard house, DeeDee noticed a friend of Tito's on the deck of the boat calling to him frantically. It seemed odd, but she didn't think much about it until she realized he was trying to signal Tito that she had arrived. When she went below deck she found Tito having sex with a waitress who worked at the coffee shop down the street from their Encino home.

The family was in an uproar over Tito's behavior. He made no attempt to apologize; instead, he rationalized his behavior by saying DeeDee was reluctant to have sex with him. In response, DeeDee voiced a complaint common among the Jackson wives. "Tito wants sex three or four times a day," she told me. "There comes a time in life when your responsibilities change. You need to direct your attention to your children. Sex is fine, but it is hardly the first thing that comes into my mind morning, noon, and night."

She said Tito would often sit up in bed and scream that he wanted sex NOW. Her feelings were immaterial, DeeDee revealed. "If I said no, we would have a major fight. If I said yes, I felt cheapened and controlled. It was a no-win situation that had to stop."

Tito continued his affair. One night I received a call from Katherine, who told me she had just heard from a friend of DeeDee's named Lisa Jones. DeeDee had been visiting Lisa and had had too much to drink. Katherine asked me to go with her to pick up DeeDee and bring her over to Hayvenhurst for the night. DeeDee sat in the backseat of the car, crying uncontrollably. I felt badly for her because she seemed so miserable and had given up all hope of ever resuming her marriage. When we arrived at Hayvenhurst, I took her into the guest room and told her I would keep her company that night.

It was like a slumber party. We stayed up most of the night and talked. She kept repeating one thing to me over and over. "Margaret, put something away for a rainy day. I know that you and Jermaine are very much in love now, but you never know. I'm telling you that the day will come, as it has for all the wives."

I knew then that I had to prepare for life on my own.

Several days later, DeeDee Martes Jackson filed for divorce from Torinao Adaryll Tito Jackson after eighteen years of marriage. The entire family was saddened by the news, with the exception of Tito. He disappeared for a period of time, cutting off not only his wife, but all his children as well.

The perfect Jackson marriage had ended, and I was taking a hard look at my own relationship. I watched as the family sided immediately with Tito, saying that they really couldn't blame him for looking outside for sex, since DeeDee was "withholding."

It was bad enough when Tito didn't make court-appointed alimony payments, but it was unconscionable when he decided to stop funding his sons' tuition to Buckley School, where fees run upward of $10,000 a year. Tito's sons are extremely bright and were getting straight A's. DeeDee was frantic that her sons were going to have to leave school. Then Uncle Michael got wind of what was happening, and paid for all of them to go through Buckley and is now funding their college education.

Tito's marriage wasn't the only one to end in divorce during 1990. Eliza Shaffe Jackson soon filed for divorce from Steven Randall Jackson. Those two had always had a love-hate relationship, but when Eliza filed she also lodged a criminal complaint against Randy for beating her. She charged he had beaten her when she was pregnant with their daughter, Stevanna. Although Randy maintained his innocence, he pleaded no contest to the charges and was sentenced to two years' probation, including weekly counseling sessions.

At the same time Marlon, who was still happily married to Carol, ran into serious financial difficulties. They were having trouble paying the

$7,000 mortgage and property tax bills on their house. Despite a $60,000 loan from Katherine, Marlon and Carol eventually lost their home and moved into a small place in San Diego.

In May 1990 Marlon auctioned off his possessions. Among the items he sold were his costumes and jacket from the *Victory* tour, his gold records, his paintings and statues, and his two championship rings, which were formerly owned by Muhammad Ali and Sugar Ray Leonard. Janet also moved to San Diego that year with her boyfriend, René Elizondo. She lived in a six-bedroom home estimated to have cost $4 million. Janet, the sister all the brothers had vetoed when she wanted to participate in the *Victory* tour, had long since passed them on the ladder of success.

Over the next several months, Jermaine continued to travel. On one trip Lea Bongo accompanied him to Africa. Lea had had an argument with Madam and had been sent packing back to her homeland. Jermaine was going to Africa to join Madam in concert as a way of helping to launch her singing career. After the concert, Jermaine continued to meet with Wallace Farrakhan, the son of Nation of Islam leader Louis Farrakhan, and traveled to Ghana in support of the elder Farrakhan, who was giving a speech there. Jermaine seemed to be drifting deeper into the Islam beliefs.

Back on the home front, I was given the responsibility of moving once again. Because Jermaine's new record producers, L.A. and Baby-Face, lived in Atlanta, we were moving across the country to become Georgia's newest residents. I was supposed to fly to Atlanta, find us a house, rent the house, come back, and pack up and move the kids, furniture, dishes, Range Rover, Corniche, and everything. And that's just what I did.

When Jermaine returned from Africa, I met him at the airport and drove him to his beautiful new Georgian-style home in an affluent suburb called Buckhead on the same street where the governor lived. The house was so large that not even all our furniture could fill the place. I ended up having to rent roomfuls of furniture so the house wouldn't look bare. It was close to Christmas and I had a lovely tree, fully decorated, in the living room. The logs were burning in the fireplace, a turkey was in the oven, and the Jermaine Jackson family was reunited in true Hallmark Card style.

The day after he returned from his trip, Jermaine mentioned that he thought he must have bathed in dirty bathwater in Africa, or perhaps that he had been in an unclean bathroom. He told me he felt a burning and irritating sensation when he urinated. I didn't think much about it at the time. A couple of days later, however, I began to notice that something wasn't quite right with me either. Since I was new in Atlanta and had no family doctor in the area, I was in a bit of a panic. I turned to Jermaine's lawyer, Joel Katz, and his wife, Kane, who lived nearby. Sensing the urgency in my voice, Kane offered to drive me to her doctor. When Jermaine found out where I was headed, he insisted on coming along.

The doctor examined me and said he could find nothing wrong. I told him to test me again. After the second examination and another look under the microscope, the doctor found that I indeed had an infection. He stammered and stuttered his way through the diagnosis before deciding I had a rare African bacteria, fortunately treatable with antibiotics. I thought he went out of his way to tell me it was not contracted through sex. At that point I cared less about what it was than about how to get rid of it. He gave Jermaine and me some pills and sent us both home.

That night I got a phone call from Kane.

"I've just spoken to the doctor," she said. "The doctor was too scared to tell you. You don't have a rare African disease. You've got gonorrhea.

And you got it from Jermaine. He was making threatening gestures to the doctor behind your back, holding his fist up. Jermaine gave you gonorrhea. He must have brought it home from Africa."

I thanked Kane despite my embarrassment, having moved through the emotions of shock, then anger, then humiliation. I hung up the phone and went into the living room, where Jermaine was sitting.

"You know, Jermaine, this was a wonderful Christmas present you brought home to me," I said, struggling to keep my composure. "It's bad enough you had sex, but you're an idiot for not using protection. You could have exposed this entire family to AIDS."

If I had expected the father of my children to apologize, I could have saved my breath. Jermaine told me that the doctor was lying. He did the famous Jackson sidestep and this time put the blame on Kane and Joel, saying he thought they wanted to break the two of us up.

I stared at him, weighing my options carefully. The thought of killing him didn't enter my head, but that was about the only scenario that didn't. There was no way he was going to admit that he had sex or that he had gonorrhea. I left the room. DeeDee's warning came back to haunt me: "You never know. I'm telling you that the day will come, as it has for all the wives."

That night I called Katherine and unburdened myself on her. She listened carefully and compassionately.

"I only wish he had admitted it, said he made a mistake, apologized. Then we could have moved on," I said as calmly as I could, my voice shaking. "Instead, he lied to me, Katherine. He must think I'm some kind of idiot if he thinks that I'm going to believe that he visited a dirty bathroom in Africa and came home with a venereal disease!"

There was a pause on the other end, followed by a sigh. Katherine told me how sorry she was that I had to go through this. She said she understood my feelings. "Joseph did the same thing to me back in the Gary, Indiana, days," she said.

Katherine said that, like me, she didn't know what was wrong, saw a doctor, and then confronted Joseph, who denied any knowledge of either having the disease or spreading it.

Even though Katherine's admission was touching, it didn't make me feel any better. Neither did her advice to pack my bags and the kids and return to Encino for a while. I remembered her earlier advice to me not to run from a problem, so I thanked her, and declined her offer of escape. I thought about letting Jermaine's transgression slide but convinced myself that I had let too many things slide without expressing my feelings. The more I brought up the gonorrhea incident, the more obstinate Jermaine became. Finally he directed his attack at me.

"How do I know that you're not the one who gave me the disease?" he asked. "You were here in Atlanta by yourself the entire time while I was gone."

I was furious. He knew I didn't know any men in Atlanta and that I'd spent the entire time he was gone moving children, furniture, and cars to take the pressure off of him. He knew I'd never once given him any reason to suspect that I would or could ever have an affair. After I reminded him of all this, he came up with a new one. He accused me of fooling around with Kane Katz's sixteen-year-old nephew. I was too disgusted to respond.

I tried to figure a way out of the situation, keeping in mind what had happened to the other wives. I knew Enid wasn't getting her child support and had been cut off completely by the family. I knew Hazel wouldn't have gotten any child support if it wasn't for my intervention and that of Howard Grossman. I had seen Tito and

DeeDee break up and had witnessed the whole family turning their backs on the wife who had been their favorite. And I knew Randy was on probation for beating Eliza. But it wasn't time to leave yet. I needed a plan.

I put my personal concerns aside so that Jermaine could begin work on his album, then we discovered that he was getting the brush-off by L.A. Face Records. They seemed to be coming up with excuse after excuse for postponing the start of the recording sessions. I took matters into my own hands and telephoned Vernon Schlatter, the president of L.A. Face, to ask when Jermaine would be going into the studio. He said everyone was out of town and that he would get back to me. Three months went by with no word. Finally I called again. This time I was told that L.A. and BabyFace were in Los Angeles working with Michael Jackson on his new album, *Dangerous*.

It was a bombshell. Jermaine was more than hurt; he was furious. Michael knew how excited Jermaine was and that we had moved to Atlanta specifically to work with these producers. "He could have any producers he wanted!" Jermaine screamed. "Why does he have to take the two who were working with me?"

The answer is that Michael wanted the best in the business, and the best wanted to work with him. Even a single hit on a Michael Jackson album could earn them millions of dollars. A hit on a Jermaine Jackson album had little chance of doing the same. In a way, I couldn't blame Michael. He was being a shrewd businessman and, as anyone involved in the record business knows, this sort of thing goes on all the time.

When L.A. and BabyFace finally returned to Atlanta, it was with empty pockets. Michael Jackson hadn't used any of their material on his new album, so they headed into the studio with Jermaine. The first song they recorded was a single entitled "Word to the Badd!"

It was the song in which Jermaine lambasted his brother Michael and created a rift that continues to this day.

8

When I first heard the lyrics to Jermaine's "Word to the Badd!" I was saddened but hardly surprised. Jermaine's jealousy of his brother had hit epic proportions by mid-1991.

"Reconstructed / Been abducted / Don't know who you are. . . . Once you were made / You changed your shade / Was your color wrong? / Could not turn back / It's a known fact / You were too far gone. . . ." The song had a decent track, but the lyrics were so vile that I initially thought it was some sort of sick joke. Surely Jermaine had no intention of releasing a record in which he lambasted his brother for neglecting his family, lightening his skin color, and having plastic surgery. It was scary. It got even scarier when Jermaine told me that was exactly what he was going to do.

He had written the song to put Michael in his place. Jermaine thought the song was the best thing he had ever done. When I asked Jermaine if he thought a song like that could ever make it on his record, his response was, "I don't know, but I want it to." With that one song recorded, Jermaine seemed to go into overdrive. Driven by sibling rivalry, he completed his *You Said* album for L.A. Face in record time.

In March 1991 Janet had astounded many in the music business with the huge deal she signed with Richard Branson at Virgin Records. While Janet had been a successful artist for A&M Records (press releases refer to her as the biggest selling artist in the company's history), the expiration of her deal in 1990 caused a bidding war for her talents that few could have predicted.

It was going to take a fistful of cash to get Janet to sign on a new dotted line and the heads of A&M, Capitol, Atlantic, and Virgin all knew it. When the dust settled, the actual figures were staggering. Virgin Records signed a three-album deal with the Jacksons' youngest daughter that would pay her $30 million, plus a 22 percent royalty on the retail price of each album. At that figure Janet surpassed even her brother Michael in contract value. Virgin was paying a hefty price to establish itself as a major player in the recording industry. It had just put out its open-for-business sign in the United States four years earlier. Until the time Janet signed with Virgin, the company's top female recording star was Paula Abdul, Jackie's former girlfriend.

Michael also had a new deal to announce. He politely waited for Janet to have her moment in the sun, then allowed Sony Inc. to call its own press conference. Michael Jackson had just re-signed with the label for $60 million, plus 25 percent royalties on the retail price of each album. Additionally, he would get his own label, which he called M.J.J. Records.

The two deals were astronomical, and no one took the news harder than Jermaine. When he looked at the multimillions his brother and sister were earning, the estimated $1 million he might ultimately receive for his latest album, *You Said,* seemed rather weak.

Since he couldn't compete on a monetary level, Jermaine was determined to do so on an artistic level. He spent more and more of his days and some of his nights in the recording studio. In the meantime I continued to devote my attention to the miniseries. Shortly after I had received the first draft of the shooting script from screenwriter

Joyce Eliason, Katherine called with the news that Joseph had had a stroke. The news was unsettling. Katherine had always said that Joseph was "too evil to die." It seemed now that maybe that wasn't true.

Joseph visited us in Atlanta after he had recovered, and I could see that he had quieted down. I remember handing him the miniseries script to read. He refused it, handing it back to me with a shake of his head. "I'm sure it's fine, Margaret," he said. In the old days he would have given the script to one of his flunkies to read and then argued over every other word.

That summer Dawn and her mother reappeared. They both came over to our Buckhead house, and I took the opportunity to tell Dawn's mother that the party was over.

"Jermaine doesn't have the kind of money he used to have," I told the woman while Dawn sat and listened. "Don't expect any more to be coming your way." Neither Dawn nor her mother put up much of a fight. Actually, there was very little they could say. I had made it clear that I was now controlling the checkbook and the checkbook was closed.

By September 1991 we were heading back to California. Nothing more was said about "Word to the Badd!" and I certainly was not about to bring it up. I had been spending hours on the phone talking with Katherine about the miniseries, taking care of the nuts and bolts of preproduction on *The Jacksons: An American Dream*. The five-hour-long form had been sold to the ABC television network for a whopping $10 million, $1 million of which went to the family for the rights to the story.

Because only Katherine and Joseph were now living at Hayvenhurst, Jermaine and I were offered our old room back with an extra perk: Katherine told us she would open up LaToya's room to us as well. Since I anticipated working with Katherine on the miniseries anyway, it made sense to call Hayvenhurst our home once again.

LaToya was gone but not forgotten. She had seen to that by releasing her book *LaToya*. It was the book the family had been hearing about and fearing for months; the book that was being billed as "the most shocking and stirring showbiz story ever told." More correctly, it was a distortion of the truth in LaToya's effort to attract desperately needed attention.

Much has been written about LaToya and her memoir. What was interesting to me was that the wildest story wasn't in the book at all, but rather was planted by LaToya's husband and manager, Jack Gordon, in *Rolling Stone* magazine. The story quoted him as saying that Michael Jackson had offered LaToya $5 million not to write the book and she'd declined. It gave family members a big laugh. If Michael had offered his sister that kind of money, everyone said, she would have the cash in her pocket and a padlock on the manuscript.

The real story is far more interesting.

When LaToya had just begun to outline her memoir, soon after leaving Hayvenhurst back in 1988, Jack approached Jerome Howard, Joseph's business partner, with an offer he wanted to pass along to Katherine. The deal was simple: If Katherine would pay Jack Gordon $5 million, he would see to it that no book was ever published. Jack even offered Jerome a cut.

Without accepting a percentage for himself, Jerome took Jack's offer to Katherine, who was repulsed by the entire plan, labeling it outright extortion. The other family members agreed and pushed Katherine into reporting it to the authorities. She met with agents from the Los Angeles Bureau of the FBI and told them about Jack Gordon's extortion plot. In an effort to ensure an airtight case against him, the FBI wanted Katherine to set up a meeting with Jack and wear a wire. At first Katherine was willing to go along with the plan, since it seemed an excellent way to rid the family and LaToya of Gordon's influence, but she eventually backed off because she was afraid Gordon would retaliate. Jack would later try to present the same deal to Michael with even less success.

Despite the fact that the family found LaToya's book to be offensive and scandalous, the truth is that much of what LaToya had to say was not that far from wrong.

Once the book was published, LaToya was like a woman unleashed. With each new interview, each new talk show, she added stories to the ones in the book, lurid tales of physical, emotional, and sexual abuse. Katherine had to sit and watch as her favorite daughter claimed on talk show after talk show that Joseph had put guns to their heads as children and whipped them within an inch of their lives. LaToya also claimed that her father had molested her sister Rebbie and tried to molest her. Rebbie vehemently denied that story and refused to discuss it further with anyone.

At the same time LaToya's book was making the rounds, Joyce Eliason was putting the finishing touches on the script for the miniseries. It was quite a paradox to watch Katherine deny in the press that Joseph had ever struck their children, then read transcripts of interviews with Joyce in which Katherine had spoken of just such incidents. The interview that still haunts me was one that came from Jackie. While all the brothers made references to Joseph's temper and the beatings they would receive at his hand, Jackie, as the oldest boy, saw and felt more than any of the others.

"My father used to hurt," Jackie told Joyce. "I mean, if you knew you had a beating the next morning, you couldn't sleep at night. We were scared of him—all of us. Especially when I was little. We would all try hard in school and if we got bad grades, he would line us up on our knees and hit us.

"I remember we studied the time tables on Saturdays and we'd be shaking. Even if we knew them, we'd be shaking 'cause you're thinking about the beating if you miss one. And if you did, he'd get a switch off a tree and pull down your pants.

"He was hard on us, all right. Too hard. I always thought maybe he was upset 'cause he worked so hard and he was taking it out on us a little bit. My father was the type of guy, he never showed us love. He loved us, but he never showed it.

"He never put his arms around us and said,

'Son, I love you.' My father never said 'I love you,' ever, to any of us. I never got that from him.

"My son knows that I love him. When I think about it, it brings tears to my eyes all the time 'cause my father just couldn't say that. I know that he really wanted to, but he never could say those words, 'I love you, son.'"

With the memory of that interview and others in my mind, I watched as Joseph would repeatedly look the press straight in the eye and swear: "We never beat LaToya or any of the kids." He'd then retreat behind the gates of his home and watch all his children walk the opposite way.

In November 1991 Michael was about to release the album *Dangerous,* for which he had been paid $18 million by Sony Records plus 25 percent of the retail price for every copy sold. Everyone was expecting a blockbuster and, as usual, Michael was not about to disappoint.

"Word to the Badd!" was mysteriously leaked to a radio station in Los Angeles several days before "Black or White's" official release. Both singles, "Black or White" and "Word to the Badd!" were dropped off separately in the early evening at the same radio station in brown paper bags. No note; no instructions.

The station played both records, first "Black or White," then "Word to the Badd!" Over and over, those were the only two songs the disc jockey played. The telephone at Hayvenhurst began to ring as friends and business associates heard "Badd" and reacted.

Jermaine walked around strutting like a peacock. In his entire career, he had never had his music played so much on the air. He was invigorated by the controversy and loved the intrigue of how the songs were leaked. Clive Davis, president of Arista Records, was less than pleased, as was Jermaine's producer.

The following morning at 10 o'clock, Michael came up the driveway of the Hayvenhurst house. We watched his arrival from our bedroom window. Jermaine seemed to welcome the opportunity to confront Michael face-to-face. When L.A. and BabyFace had disappeared from Atlanta and we discovered they were working for Michael, Jermaine made repeated attempts to contact his brother. None of his calls was ever returned. This was his moment to speak to Michael and he seemed ready for anything. Other published accounts of this confrontation suggest that Michael and Jermaine came to blows in the driveway between the guard gate and the recording studio. It was said that Michael physically attacked Jermaine, promising to "kick ass." Nothing could be further from the truth.

When Michael entered the house, he and Jermaine went into the trophy room off the foyer and closed the door. A second later Katherine went in to mediate their discussion.

Thoughts were racing through my head as I waited for an explosion. First, I knew we would be kicked out of the house; after all, Michael was paying for everything—the phones, the cars, the cooks, the maids, the security, the gardeners, the pool men, the maintenance men, everything!

Then I remembered the miniseries. I knew Michael would never sign off on anything we did from that point on. And the way the contracts had been negotiated, he had approval over everything.

Our agent, Rob Lee, telephoned. "How could Jermaine do this now? Michael could pull the plug on the whole miniseries," Rob yelled into his speakerphone. I told Rob I'd call him back as soon as I knew anything. As far as I could tell, they weren't yelling, they weren't fighting. I could hear nothing but silence, and an occasional thump as if someone had banged his hand on the table.

The telephone rang again. It was Clive Davis. "Margaret, what's going on?" he asked. I had to tell him what I had told Rob Lee. Basically, I didn't know anything, but said I'd call him the second the meeting broke up.

The next call came from Jermaine's attorney, Joel Katz, in Atlanta. He had heard about the record on the news. "What's going on? I heard this song has been leaked to radio. What, has Jermaine gone nuts? He's going to kill his career."

Again, I repeated my plea of ignorance and my pledge to call back as soon as I had any news. The meeting lasted a good half hour before the door to the trophy room finally opened. Michael left the house without saying a word to anyone. Soon afterward, Jermaine left as well. I immediately went running to Katherine to learn what had happened and tried to read the reaction on her face.

"I don't understand Jermaine," Katherine said to me as we settled into chairs in the kitchen. "He was so mean to Michael. Michael was crying at the way his brother was treating him. Michael kept repeating over and over, 'Why Jermaine? Why did you do it?' "

Katherine said Jermaine slammed his hand down on the table and said, "You're just mad because it's my turn now. Somebody else is getting some of the spotlight."

She said Michael just sat there and took the accusations Jermaine was handing out. When he did finally speak, it was only to repeat himself.

"I'm your brother. How could you write something like that about me?"

Jermaine never responded directly to the question, but rather talked about the fact that Michael had never called him back about the L.A.-Baby-Face affair.

"Please, Jermaine, don't release this song. It's not going to hurt my career, but it will totally ruin yours. My fans aren't going to care. Don't do it, Jermaine, for your own sake," Michael pleaded.

Jermaine wouldn't listen. Essentially, the meeting was over. Jermaine had shown absolutely no remorse. He said he wrote the song and he was going to stand by it. At that point Michael left. I could tell Katherine was embarrassed for Jermaine. She kept shaking her head and saying, "I don't know. I don't know what's gotten into the boy."

I had difficulty explaining it as well. Michael had given Jermaine a roof over his head and picked up the expenses for the entire family. He did it gladly. He also allowed us the opportunity to televise the family's life story. It had been sold to ABC mainly on the strength of the Michael Jackson name.

When Michael left, the last thing he did was give Jermaine the direct line to his trailer at the location where he was shooting his next video. He wanted Jermaine to call him and tell him that he had decided not to release the song nationwide as a single. When I learned he had the phone number, I begged Jermaine to call his brother and end the entire fiasco. I couldn't get Jermaine to believe how stupid he was being.

"Hell, no," Jermaine shouted at me. "This is what Michael needs. He needs someone like me to put some fire under his ass. To let him know that he's not the only one around here who can create some heat. He's just scared because he knows that I'm going to happen this time. He'd better watch out for his brother, Jermaine."

Jermaine never called Michael. Later in the day, the telephone rang and when I answered it, Michael was on the other end of the line. He asked to speak to Jermaine, who told me to tell Michael that he wasn't around.

Michael could only let his brother dig his own grave. He didn't try to retaliate legally or any other way. As it turned out, he didn't have to. Clive Davis at Arista was not about to allow "Word to the Badd!" on an album if it included lyrics demeaning to a superstar like Michael Jackson. "Word to the Badd!" ended up on the album *You Said* but with a totally different theme. This time the lyrics were about the relationship between Jackie and Paula Abdul. The original version was briefly released but turned out to be more of a novelty than a bestseller and was quickly withdrawn.

Somehow I knew I was going to be blamed for the whole debacle. The spouses always took the heat from the family for whatever was happening. When LaToya messed up, it was all because of Jack Gordon. When Marlon stopped coming around, the family blamed Carol for putting a voodoo curse on him. When Jermaine and Hazel got into money trouble, it was Hazel's fault. When Tito started cheating on DeeDee, it was DeeDee's fault. It was my turn to take the fall.

I didn't find out until later that Katherine blamed me for the song, even though she knew I had nothing whatsoever to do with it. In her eyes, however, her children could do no wrong. There's always an outside reason, she felt, and she somehow convinced everyone that I was it.

The "Word to the Badd!" situation came and went quickly, leaving a horrible taste in the mouths of Jermaine's fans, who couldn't understand why he would turn against his brother. His *You Said* album got lost in the dust of Michael's *Dangerous* album. One single after another was released, each supported by brilliantly produced videos. The more Michael's career soared, the more Jermaine's went straight into the toilet. And right behind it was our relationship.

We were just politely cohabiting. After the gonorrhea episode in Atlanta, I had difficulty maintaining an active sexual life with Jermaine. We discussed it and I explained to him why, and it didn't make the reality any less frustrating for him. Not only was I unsure that he wasn't going to infect me with something else, but I also never forgot the fact that he didn't apologize for cheating on me while he was on the road. If he did it once, he could do it hundreds of times and I would have absolutely no way of knowing.

Jermaine became more and more sexually demanding as I became increasingly disinterested in him. He went to his mother and begged her to intercede. Katherine came to me for another one of our heart-to-hearts.

She sat me down and told me that as a wife it was part of my "duty" to sleep with my husband. I told her I was taking care of our two kids, producing a miniseries, and trying to help Jermaine with his career since he refused to get a manager. I told her I was not the twenty-year-old girl he first met, who was perfectly content to have sex day and night. Things change in relationships. And this was definitely a change. In truth, I was beginning to realize I had a mind of my own and didn't need to get my marching orders from Jermaine. The loss of control was driving him crazy.

I began to value my relationship with Katherine more than the one I had with her son. I saw her—I *wanted* to see her—as a solid and centered rock to which we all clung. Nothing fazed her or was beyond her wisdom.

About this time, another family tragedy struck. Jackie had been dating a wealthy woman named Shadow. It was a volatile relationship that ultimately ended when, after an argument with Jackie, Shadow took a large quantity of sleeping pills and died. We were shocked by her death and felt worse when we learned that Jackie's son, Siggie, discovered the body the following day.

As we began to work full-time on the miniseries, I heard more of Katherine's family stories. She had released her own book about the family called *The Jacksons: My Family,* written with Richard Wiseman. In it she glossed over many of the stories that she now seemed only too eager to tell me. Some were enlightening, some were petty. None, however, had the impact of the Gina Sprague story. Although we were trying to be truthful in the script, this was one story we decided not to put on the small screen.

9

Gina Sprague's involvement with the Jackson family began when she started working as a receptionist in Joseph's management office on Sunset Boulevard in the same high-rise building that housed Motown Records. It was late 1979, and she was nineteen years old. A year later, Gina's job would come to an end in dramatic fashion at the hands of Katherine.

Gina was a dancer who had attracted Joseph's eye while she was performing with the Jeff Kutash dance troupe. She gained an entry into show business by winning a contest on the TV show "American Bandstand" in 1978. For years Katherine had been tolerant of Joseph's wandering eye. Joseph flaunted his girlfriends in front of his sons when they performed on the road as the Jackson 5, but never in front of Katherine. So, for Katherine, it was out of sight, out of mind.

Gina Sprague was different. Although she never admitted to having a sexual relationship with Joseph, Gina made the mistake of insinuating herself into Katherine's home life. She would call the Hayvenhurst house frequently to talk with Joseph and, more often than not, Katherine would pick up the phone. Gina said the calls were business; Katherine knew they were personal. Katherine had always told me that a wife knows when another woman is sleeping with her husband, and she knew Gina was sleeping with Joseph.

Joseph made no secret of his fondness for the slim, attractive girl. He absorbed her hand-fed compliments like newspaper in a kennel and bought into her opinion that he, and only he, was responsible for the enormous success of the Jackson family. So close did the two become that Joseph even took Gina to meet Cheryl Terrell, the mother of his daughter Joh' Vonnie. In short order Gina was promoted to Joseph's personal assistant and was responsible for a variety of tasks, including keeping Joseph Jackson happy.

Gina's flaunting of her relationship with Joseph ended up being more than Katherine could take. On October 15, 1980, Katherine phoned Gina to tell her to clean out her desk and get out of their lives.

"Get out, or I'm gonna get you," Katherine is supposed to have screamed.

The next day Katherine went to Joe Jackson Productions on Sunset Boulevard to make certain Gina knew she meant business. She was not alone. She had brought backup in the form of Janet, then age fourteen, and Randy, then eighteen. They meant business as well.

Randy is said to have entered the office first, asking several employees to leave so that he could speak with Gina alone. When they complied, Janet joined her brother and got into a heated argument with Gina about her relationship with their father. When Katherine entered the office, Janet grabbed Gina's wrist to hold her in place. Katherine attacked Gina, pulling her hair and screaming, "I told you I was gonna get you, bitch."

There are several versions of this story, but all of them end the same way. Randy knocked Gina to the ground, and all three dragged the woman from the office, beating her about the face and head. People in the building heard Gina's screams and came to her aid. They were first told to stay out of it. "This is family business," Janet is alleged to have said. As more and more bystanders gawked in disbelief, the Jackson trio made a getaway down the elevator and disappeared.

As Gina limped back into the office, Joseph, who had been in a meeting, was stunned to see her dress torn, her face bruised. An ambulance arrived, summoned by the building's security guard. Gina was rushed to Hollywood Presbyterian Medical Center, where she was treated for cuts and bruises to her head and face. She was released the following day.

When Michael heard the story, he refused to believe a word of it. Even now, there is nothing that could convince him that it took place. Yet it's a story that Katherine told freely as we sat on our favorite chairs on the landing at the top of the stairs.

"Randy and Janet and I went to his office and I beat her," Katherine readily admitted. "This woman was screwing around with Joseph and it just got to be too much. I told her to quit her job, but the woman wouldn't leave. So I went there and beat the daylights out of her."

Katherine had a habit of chewing on the inside of her lip when she got angry, and she was working her cheek pretty well as she related the story.

"I will not put up with that stuff," she stated frankly. "I will not tolerate it for a minute. I'll knock somebody's head off first." That day in October, Katherine nearly did.

Gina Sprague sued Katherine, Joseph, Randy, and Janet for $21 million and was effectively blackballed in the close-knit entertainment community. The lawsuit was eventually settled out of court. To this day Gina claims to have never received any money from the Jacksons and denies ever having slept with Joseph. She is quoted as having a message for Katherine, however: "If I could talk to Mrs. Jackson right now, I'd tell her the next time her husband is hoochie-shoochie some other woman, hit *him*, not the woman."

Gina's sentiments have been echoed many times before and since outside of the Jackson family. No matter the problem or the consequence, the Jacksons were always the innocents. The world is forever in a feeding frenzy around them, while they themselves can do no wrong. I knew I could expect no better treatment, regardless of how much I tried to prove I was really on their side.

With Jermaine's recording career at a standstill, he announced he wasn't content with being an "artist" any longer. He said artists are merely hired hands. He wanted to be the boss—the producer, the director, the studio owner. He was continuing to fly to New Jersey for meetings with Bob Petrallia, whose ideas for Jackson Communications Inc. (JCI) were growing even larger. I always thought that you have to crawl before you can walk, so I didn't believe anything Bob Petrallia promised to deliver, and he never did deliver anything. At the time, however, Jermaine needed to feel like a big shot, and being head of a corporation seemed to allow him that.

Bob Petrallia had asked Jermaine and me to fly to Switzerland, where he said JCI was "in the acquisition stage" (his favorite phrase) of buying a television station. As I was packing for the trip, I learned we would be taking one additional person along for the ride: Lea Bongo.

Jermaine wanted Lea along on the trip because she spoke five languages, and all the negotiations were being done in French. Taking Lea along wasn't as simple as it sounded, though. Lea had gotten into trouble with her half-sister, Madam. According to Madam, Lea had taken her American Express card without permission and shopped up and down Rodeo Drive. Madam was not pleased when the total topped $10,000, and she wasted little time in letting Lea know it. Madam was a strict disciplinarian who was used to running an entire country. It didn't take much

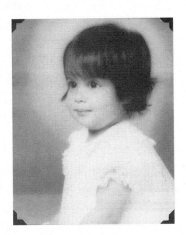

Me as a baby.

My brother Willie Maldonado (age 4) and me (age 5).
He calls this our Lucy and Ricky photo.

Me at age 15 going on 35.

Me at 15 in Las Vegas.

Me in New York at age 17
heading for the fast lane.

My mom, Joan Maldonado-Gius, a hot number in 1978.

My mom, the school teacher;
I'm so proud of her. 1995.

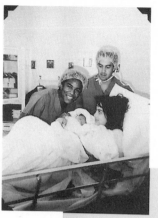

Jermaine, my brother
Willie, and me the day
I had Jeremy. 1986.

Jermaine with one day
old Jeremy.

Jourdynn at age 2.

Jermaine and me catching
the train in Germany. I
was so in love. 1987.

Jermaine and me in Africa
in 1987. I am wearing an
African wedding necklace.

Jermaine and me
in Africa in 1987.

Jeremy and Brooke Shields at a concert in Korea where Jermaine was performing.

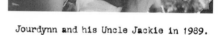

Jourdynn and his Uncle Jackie in 1989.

Jermaine and Jeremy at a photo shoot in 1989.

Jermaine with his four sons:
Jermaine Jr., Jaimy, Jourdynn, and Jeremy.

T.J., Jermaine Jr., Jeremy, Siggy, Tarrel, Austin, and
Taj at photo shoot for "2300 Jackson Street" in 1989.

Jermaine
and me
with his
mysterious
"daughter"
Dawn. 1989.

Jermaine's first and
second wives: Hazel
Gordy Jackson and me.

(courtesy Janet Factor)

DeeDee, Katherine, clothes designer
Pari Malek, Rebbie, and me.

Jeremy fancies
himself a
poolman at
Uncle
Michael's
jacuzzi.

Jeremy with his Uncle
Jackie outside Michael's
bedroom in 1989.

Tito and the late
DeeDee Jackson. 1989.

Jeremy and his half-brother Jaimy.

Michael's giraffe,
Jabbar, who ate
the tree tops at
Hayvenhurst.

Jermaine Jr., Jermaine,
me, and Autumn at
Wembley Stadium.

Jermaine and our
son Jeremy.

DeeDee with the actor who played Tito in the miniseries.

Katherine fussing about something in the miniseries to me.

Jermaine, Randy, Katherine, Tito, Jackie. 1989.

Jermaine, Jeremy, Jourdynn, and me on the set during the filming of the miniseries "The Jacksons: An American Dream."

Jermaine, Jackie, and Tito in Paris promoting the "2300 Jackson Street" album.

Katherine with all her grandchildren except Marlon and Carol's kids. Marlon and Carol had already distanced themselves from the family. 1989.

Joseph, Michael, and Jackie's son Siggy during "2300 Jackson Street" video shoot.

Katherine and Joseph.

Family video
shoot. 1989.

Jeremy with his Uncle Tito
and our business manager
Howard Grossman. 1992.

Jermaine and me going to
a black tie event where
Janet was getting an
American Cinema Award.

Jeremy and Jourdynn in
front of grandmother's
Rolls on their first
day at school.

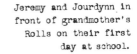

Jourdynn, Jeremy, Jaimy.

Alijandra with her two
children by Randy,
Randy Jr., and Genevieve.

One of the security guards
at the Jackson House.

Randy and Randy Jr.

The lovely
Lea Bongo. 1993.

Jermaine singing "You
are so beautiful..."
to Madam Bongo on
her birthday.

And yes,
Madam Bongo's
diamond necklace
is real.

Jeremy, Jourdynn, and me
at the beach in 1993.

Jermaine in "GQ" pose
in picture taken by my
brother Willie in 1990.

Me with my sons, Jeremy and Jourdynn,
and our dog, Oscar. 1995.

to get her upset. Lea had managed to do the job *really* well.

When we spoke to Lea on the telephone, she would come up with horrendous stories of abuse at the hands of Madam. There were constant claims of beatings, but they paled in comparison to the "burn torture" saga. According to Lea, Madam had taken a pot of boiling water and thrown it at her, burning her severely on the hip, shoulder, and side of her body. After living with the Jacksons, few things still sent chills through me. This tale did. I believed Lea when she said she lived in fear of Madam Bongo, who was planning on shipping her back to Gabon "to acquire some discipline." Typically, what Madam wanted, Madam got, but not this time. When Madam heard about Jermaine's plan to take Lea to Switzerland with us, she was livid. I had visions of Madam sending the African militia after us if we even tried to jet Lea out from under her jurisdiction and begged Jermaine not to get involved.

"How could you be so selfish and cruel, Margaret?" Jermaine responded, totally ignoring the Madam Bongo factor. Warning flags were flying everywhere, but I seemed to be the only one seeing them. Lea had allegedly stolen thousands of dollars and now the Jacksons were helping her to leave the country. It had all the elements of another adventure with a disastrous end.

If nothing else, Madam would simply disown Lea, making her our responsibility. For life, maybe. The more I tried to talk sense to him, the more he dug in his heels. The following weekend, Jermaine, Lea, and I took off for Switzerland.

There wasn't a moment when Lea was happy, the sole exception being her time alone with Jermaine. Whenever they were in meetings and she could play at being his assistant, she seemed to have a purpose. Outside of those times, the girl was a wreck. She was particularly unhappy during those hours when Jermaine and I were alone in our hotel room. Lea had the adjoining room and I could hear her crying. I felt awful. At one point I couldn't take it anymore and I went to her room to try to comfort her. I told her that if she couldn't remain in the United States with Madam, perhaps we could find a way for her to live at the Jackson compound or in her own apartment. I was trying to be a friend.

As much as I meant the offer, Lea knew she couldn't live in the same city as Madam and ignore the wishes of her powerful half-sister. She told me she had spoken to Madam and had agreed to her demands to return to Gabon. I was eventually the one who drove her to the airport after Jermaine's business was concluded. Tears flooded Lea's eyes as she stepped onto the plane.

The deal with the Swiss over buying a television station remains a mystery to me. As far as my own business affairs were concerned, I could handle accountants, lawyers, network executives, writers, and producers and have no trouble understanding the deals we were making. Jermaine's business, however, I never understood. Perhaps it's because Jermaine's businesses were illusions rather than reality. They were forever changing, always on the verge of being completed, and never happening. I credit the major smoke and mirrors to Bob Petrallia. He never had a problem with anything. There was not one deal where there was not also a hint of trouble. Even when I *knew* there was trouble, this man said it wasn't so.

Their business partners in Switzerland were a strange and boring group. I hated having to go to dinner with them and watch them eat steak tartare, the blood from the meat dripping off their plates. There was no way I could have lasted the entire trip. I needed a break, so I boarded an overnight train to Paris. Compared to the craziness with the Swiss, it was nice to be in the City of Lights. I checked into the Plaza Athénée. I not only wanted to escape from Jermaine's business partners, but also needed some time to consider my own priorities. I resolved to be independent and self-secure. And soon.

Once we were back in California, life quickly returned to standard lunacy at the Jackson compound. Lea was on the telephone to the Hayvenhurst house from the moment we crossed the threshold. Jermaine spent hours counseling the girl long-distance. I was working on the miniseries and we were starting to cast the parts.

The first crisis hit when Rebbie announced that she wanted to play the part of her mother. Rebbie is a beautiful woman and a wonderful singer. An actress she is not. But Suzanne de Passe and Stan Margulies wanted to give her every opportunity to show what she could do. An audition was arranged and Rebbie came to our offices to read. Rebbie wasn't the only one in the family who had her eyes on the role of Katherine. Victoria, Jackie's girlfriend-of-the-moment, also had her heart set on the part.

Then Angela Bassett came in to read for the role and it was like a tank rolling over a row of motorcycles. Angela had been on Broadway in *Ma Rainey's Black Bottom*, performed on the TV soap opera "The Guiding Light," did a handful of TV movies, and had scored a role in the John

Sayles feature *City of Hope*. She had just finished playing the wife of Malcolm X in Spike Lee's biofilm of the visionary leader. She would later be nominated a Best Actress Academy Award for her portrayal of Tina Turner in *What's Love Got to Do With It?* Angela blew away all the other competition. In fact, when Suzanne de Passe saw Angela's audition opposite our casting director, Jakie Brown, she was so overwhelmed by the performance that she was reduced to tears. "That doesn't often happen to me," Suzanne said.

The part went to Angela. Rebbie had to settle for her profit participation, just like all the other family members. Victoria got a role as an extra. And I concentrated on the hardest job of all; casting the kids who would play the young Jacksons. We thought it would be wonderful if we could work some of the real Jackson grandchildren into the miniseries portraying their parents or aunts and uncles at various times in their lives. Since there were eighteen grandchildren, we thought it was a distinct possibility. It didn't work out.

DeeDee and Tito's kids—Taj, Terrel, and T.J.—weren't interested and never came to the audition. Neither did Yashie and Stacy, Rebbie's kids. Rebbie's son, Austin, did show up but wasn't hired because I knew I couldn't depend on Rebbie, who is always late, to get him to the set on time. Jackie's son, Siggie, wasn't selected because his mother Enid was in an emotional turmoil attempting to collect child support, and, as a result, I couldn't depend on Siggie's availability during the entire shoot.

Jermaine's daughter, Autumn, would have been great for a role, but she had already been asked by her Aunt Janet to portray her in the feature film *Poetic Justice,* which Janet was doing for director John Singleton.

Marlon and Carol didn't want their children, Brittany, Valencia, and Marlon Jr., anywhere near the project. Alijandra brought her daughter Genevieve, but she was too young. So were Jeremy, Jourdynn, and Jaimy. They were all unable to take direction.

The only Jackson child who was cast was Jermaine Jr., who was to play his father, and that caused trouble. The rest of the family thought he was picked because Jermaine and I were producing. It wasn't true. His audition was excellent. To help him feel more comfortable with his performance, I even budgeted an acting coach for him, and he wound up doing a wonderful job.

The job of casting a little Michael Jackson was the toughest of all. We looked for weeks, but to no avail. Finally, Michael's office called and informed us they were sending over a boy to audition for the part. We were ecstatic. We mistakenly thought that if he pleased Michael, he would surely please the rest of us. When we scheduled an audition for the boy, we were shocked to walk into our office waiting room to discover that he was white! As it turned out, the boy's mother had called Michael's office and arranged for the meeting without Michael's knowledge.

It was Suzanne de Passe who came through by discovering a talented boy named Jason Weaver to play Michael during the Jackson 5 period. Alex Burrall and Wylie Draper portrayed him at other ages. Suzanne managed Jason, and didn't suggest him until the end of the casting process for fear of appearing as if she was pushing her client on the rest of us. A wonderful singer, Jason wound up doing some of the vocals in the miniseries, although for the most part we used Michael's voice.

It had been decided to shoot much of the miniseries in Pittsburgh, where we would re-create the look of Gary, Indiana, and I found myself in a frantic rush to pack and prepare for a month-long shooting schedule. I had hoped this would be Jermaine's big leap into a career in producing, now that he had declared he was no longer an "artist." He was remarkably detached, however, from almost every element of the miniseries.

His main concern seemed to be Lea, who was still in Africa. Jermaine was talking to her even more than he did when she lived in Beverly Hills. He complained to me that I wasn't being a very good friend to this girl and that I should take a more active interest in her well-being. His rationale totally escaped me but, for the sake of family harmony, I acquiesced and spoke with her the next time she called. It would later turn out to be one of the biggest mistakes I've made in my life.

10

Say what you will about Pittsburgh. I think the town has gotten a bad rap. The production company could not have asked for a warmer reception and harder workers than what we found there when we arrived to begin shooting on *The Jacksons: An American Dream*.

Our art director, Bruce Bellamy, and his team, Burton Jones and Tom Pedigo, reconstructed the Jackson home so convincingly that even Katherine had to admit that it took her back to the old days of the Jackson 5. They had built the kids' bunk beds exactly as she had described them, duplicated her kitchen down to the last fork and knife, and even managed to find a TV set that matched the original, which Joseph had bought and placed in their living room.

Katherine and Joseph arrived with great fanfare shortly after we began to shoot in April 1992. Joseph insisted on having his own security. For some reason he thought he would be mobbed for his autograph and insisted he be protected from the adoring fans, despite the fact that no one in Pittsburgh had the slightest clue who he was.

As production progressed, our stars quickly formed a cohesive team that made each workday an enjoyable experience. Lawrence Hilton-Jacobs did an incredible job portraying Joseph, showing both his dedication and his down side. Angela Bassett literally became Katherine Jackson. She limped, she reacted, she chewed her cheek in perfect duplication of the original. There was no greater compliment for Angela than the day Katherine stood mesmerized on the set and said she thought she was seeing herself in a dream. Vanessa Williams was portraying Suzanne de Passe, and when Berry Gordy heard that he said, "You had better get the other Williams to play me." He was referring, of course, to Billy Dee Williams, who not only got the role but was a joy to watch in action.

Jermaine and I had gotten a condo with room for Jeremy, Jourdynn, and Jermaine Jr. I had given my nanny, Heidi, a four-week vacation and hired a friend of Rebbie's named LaWanda Lane to take Heidi's place on the road. LaWanda previously worked at Motown Records as a receptionist. During that month of shooting, I got to know LaWanda. More important, she got to feel comfortable with me and began to talk. Because she was a friend of Rebbie's, she had often been around when Katherine and Rebbie had conversations. One of the subjects they often talked about, it seems, was me.

LaWanda told me that Katherine would make cracks about my relationship with Jermaine that were not too flattering. "Margaret's not used to money," Katherine told Rebbie and LaWanda. "She doesn't come from money like Hazel. In fact, that's why she's with Jermaine. She thinks he's got money."

The words were more than untrue, they hurt. After his money? Jermaine was broke. On top of that, if I hadn't stayed up nights trying to stretch a dollar six ways, he would have been a deadbeat dad as well. I realized for the first time that the close relationship I thought I had forged with Katherine was like everything else in the Jackson family: an illusion created for a purpose.

Midway through our shooting schedule, Hazel was invited to Pittsburgh and brought along her other two children, Autumn and Jaimy. Because Jermaine Jr. had been separated from his family for so long, the production company picked up the cost of Hazel's ticket, while Jermaine and I pitched in the money for Autumn and Jaimy's airfare.

It was an interesting experience seeing Hazel in Pittsburgh. If I ever needed proof that she was a liberated woman, I got it the day she appeared on the set dressed in black leather high-heel boots, black stretch pants, and a hot-pink halter top that showed off her tight, toned midriff. She looked hot.

At the time I was wearing my work clothes: a baggy sweatshirt and loose-fitting jeans. The comparison between the two of us couldn't have been more dramatic. The grips and cameramen stared at her, and I could see she enjoyed the attention. This girl had become her own woman—bigtime.

I reflected back on the first time I had met Hazel in person. Jermaine and I had driven his two older kids back to their home near Chatsworth and he invited me to meet his first wife. I had gone to the home many times but never could bring myself to go in. I didn't want to create an uncomfortable situation for Hazel or myself. This time, however, was different. I summoned up my courage and walked with Jermaine Jr. and Autumn into the house. My expectations of Hazel were preconceived, based on family discussions about Berry Gordy's chunky, spoiled daughter. Not so. Hazel was in perfect shape. She was friendly, outgoing, and sexily dressed in cutoff blue jeans and a pink body suit. And it was more than her figure that impressed me. She had a genuine quality about her that stood in marked contrast to the gimme-gimme girl she had been painted to be.

Over the next two years, we had developed a relationship based mainly on money. Hazel was a big concern for me, so much so that I would speak constantly to Jermaine's business manager, Howard Grossman, about alimony payments and child support. Howard, too, had incredible integrity and wanted to make sure that if the money was there, Hazel would get her cut. I made a point to call her and tell her when a check was on the way. I'd even call to tell her if a deal had been signed and how much money Jermaine would be getting. That way she would know what to expect for the children. I wanted to give her some sense of comfort, not because I was the new woman in Jermaine's life, but because I was a mother myself.

The fact that Jermaine had no concept of budgeting or saving never helped things. He thought nothing of spending when he had nothing, and taking when he should have been giving.

At first my relationship with Hazel was totally by telephone. As we got past the issue of alimony, we began talking about the babies, school, working out. Through our talks, Hazel and I had become friendly, and I began to learn more about Jermaine and why their marriage hadn't worked.

"I don't look at you as breaking up my marriage. I look at you as someone who saved my life," she had told me. She said Jermaine could be very controlling and that she was happy to be out of the relationship. I got to the point where I began to wonder if I hadn't gotten the short end of the stick in the Jermaine shuffle.

Our relationship had proven instrumental, before we went on location, in helping KJ Films gain the music rights from Berry Gordy's company for the miniseries. Berry held the rights and hadn't seemed eager to turn them over. He was preoccupied with writing his autobiography and didn't want to get involved. Whenever I had a conversation with Hazel, I would push for her to intercede. I used the logic that the quicker the miniseries happened, the quicker Jermaine would get money. The quicker Jermaine got paid, the quicker Hazel got paid.

Suzanne de Passe, as executive producer, was actually responsible for dealing with Berry, but she was going through her own negotiations with him on a separate issue. The two of them had been partnered in Gordy/dePasse Entertainment, which was in the process of being dissolved, and she didn't want to get the deals intermingled.

Getting the music rights was growing into a major problem when a birthday party conversation got everything sorted out. Hazel gave the party for Jaimy, who was turning five. Jermaine, Jeremy, Jourdynn, and I were invited for a dinner celebration at Hazel's house with Autumn and Jermaine Jr. The meal had just ended when Berry Gordy and his then wife, Grace, arrived, a present for Jaimy in hand.

I took advantage of the opportunity to pull Berry aside. It was the first time we had talked privately and I was surprised when he said he wanted me to know how wonderful it was that Hazel and I had become friends. He said he admired the mature way our relationship had developed and how kind it was of me to run interference with Jermaine on the child support issue.

I wasn't aware that he had even known that I had gone to bat repeatedly for his daughter. Since he brought it up, I mentioned that Jermaine, as well as several other Jackson brothers, were behind on their support payments because their cash flow had all but dried up. I told him that while Michael and Janet had money, the rest of the family was in financial chaos. I leveled with him about how much they needed the miniseries.

"Michael can't keep bailing them out. I'm sure you've experienced the same sort of thing with your family," I added, knowing full well that a father as wealthy as Berry was surely supporting at least a few relatives. He seemed to agree. But he still hadn't said he would sign off the music rights. The next day things changed.

Hazel called and patched her father through to my house. He wanted me to know that he had thought about what I had to say and thanked me for the way I had presented it. Berry said that he was going to meet with Suzanne and said he would see what he could do. Negotiations for the music rights began within a week.

Our agent, Rob Lee, had sold the miniseries to ABC for $10 million, but it soon proved inadequate for the production because the music rights alone would cost more than a million. We held a meeting to discuss how we could make up what would certainly be a multi-million-dollar deficit. The unasked question seemed to be: Would the Jacksons cover it? There was no way I was going to ask any of the Jacksons to make up the shortfall. The whole idea of the miniseries had been to make money for family members, not put some, or all, of them in debt. We all started looking for additional funds, but the money we needed was not forthcoming until Suzanne de Passe spoke to her contacts at Polygram. A deal was struck with Polygram to cover the deficit. All the money was now in place.

Our most difficult negotiations weren't with the network, with Polygram, or even with Berry Gordy. Our toughest bargaining came from within the family in determining how the money would be split among the Jacksons. Katherine was initially in favor of dividing the money up equally between all the kids, Joseph, and herself. One share each. One million dollars split eleven ways. Before she had a chance to tell anyone else, I objected to her logic.

"You're doing most of the work, Katherine," I tried to explain. "You're the one who has to sit through all the interviews with the writer and come to meetings with me. And you're the one who had all the kids." I told her she should get an extra share.

Katherine may be a lot of things, but dumb in business she is not. When she announced the split to her family, it was two shares for Katherine and ten shares split among Joseph, Tito, Jackie, Jermaine, Marlon, Michael, Randy, and Janet.

Plus LaToya. Even though she was estranged from the family, Katherine would not listen to any discussion of excluding her from the split. However, after numerous attempts to contact LaToya, who proved absolutely unreachable, her share was eventually tossed back into the pot and split among everyone equally.

Joseph, of course, was another problem, but not in the way I had anticipated. I originally had thought he would be a constant interference in the production, insisting on putting his ideas into play. And he probably would have, had it not been for LaToya. After she got done exposing his alleged abuse to the children, he was walking around with his tail between his legs. He took off for Las Vegas and stayed put.

The larger problem was the $3 million judgment that was still hanging over Joseph's head from his lawsuit with Gary Berwin. He couldn't have money coming in under his own name or the court would immediately take it. To cover that loose end, Katherine took charge of Joseph's share of the split.

The task of getting each of the family members to sign the contracts authorizing their life rights fell to me. I carried the deal from Rebbie to Tito, Tito to Randy, Randy to Jackie, and Jackie to Jermaine. Katherine handled Michael and Janet.

In return for signing off on their life rights, Michael and Janet, through their attorneys, had made several demands. For example, they wanted approval of the script, the screenwriter, the director, and the actors who would portray them in the miniseries, and Michael insisted that someone beautiful play his mother. We agreed; they signed.

In every negotiation, it seems there always has to be one person who holds up the entire deal for his own reasons. In this case, the person was Marlon, and his reason was simple: He objected to his mother getting a larger share of the pie than everyone else. In their lifetimes, the various Jackson family members have done both remarkable and questionable things. Marlon's decision falls into the latter. Nothing we would say would change his mind, and the entire future of the miniseries was hanging in the balance.

Eventually, Katherine had to make a trip to Marlon's home and reason with him to sign the contracts. When she returned, she was upset. Marlon had signed, but only after Katherine had begged him to cooperate.

"This is money for Joseph and me to grow old with, Marlon," she later told me she had said to Marlon. Tears were pouring down her face. She couldn't believe she had had to beg her own child to do what was right and fair.

When Jermaine heard about it, he called Marlon sneaky, adding, "You and Marlon are sneaky, Margaret, because you're both Pisces." I didn't deserve that.

I was living on the defensive, constantly having to explain my every move to each of the various family members. During production of the miniseries I had to promise to fax them changes and show them the bookkeeping. People were always calling to find out when they would get more money. The amount of hand-holding that was required was endless. The Jacksons just weren't able to trust one another.

Mother's Day fell near the end of the Pittsburgh shoot and we all went out to dinner to celebrate. Jermaine had been particularly attentive for the past week. At dinner he handed me a ring and asked me to marry him and make it official. The irony of the moment was overwhelming. I didn't know how to phrase my answer. I had concluded months before that there was absolutely no way I was going to marry Jermaine Jackson. I could see the direction he was going. He was turning into a clone of his father and the idea of being married to anyone who behaved like Joseph was unacceptable to me.

His proposal was just the beginning. He

launched a campaign to convince me to get pregnant. Even if I hadn't been midway through producing a very demanding and complicated family project, the idea wouldn't have appealed to me. I had already had two children with Jermaine, two great kids who were occupying much of my time. But enough was enough, and I told him so. Jermaine was not pleased and let me know in any number of ways. The most obvious was a change in his manner of speaking to me. Where he was once civil, he became caustic. Where he was once sweet, he became acerbic. The further we got into the miniseries, the nastier the words became.

I was emotionally out from under his thumb. The sting of that realization on Jermaine's part was compounded by another hit by his famous brother. Michael, who had stolen his glory with *Dangerous*, had one-upped Jermaine again.

The headline read: MICHAEL JACKSON CROWNED AS KING IN AFRICA. The man behind the headline: Omar Bongo, former husband of Madam.

Michael had agreed to go on a tour of Gabon at the invitation of the president and was met by more than 100,000 cheering fans; more people turned out to greet him than had greeted the pope or Nelson Mandela. Under a sacred tree, Michael was proclaimed King of Sani in the goldmining town of Krindjabo by the Agni tribe. He hugged children, visited orphanages, and prayed in the Basilica of Our Lady of Peace Church on the Ivory Coast. He showed humility, honor, poise, and affection, traits with which Jermaine had totally lost touch.

As his brother logged 30,000 miles in eleven days and touched four continents, traveling in his private Boeing 707, Jermaine was in Pittsburgh getting increasingly jealous with each newscast. Once again Jermaine had been overshadowed by his brother, this time at the hands of his "dear friends," the Bongos. While Michael was being wined and dined with gold goblets and jeweled plates at the Bongo palace, Jermaine was at home steaming, thinking that it should have been him.

After shooting wrapped in Pittsburgh in late May, the production company returned to Los Angeles, where we spent another couple of months filming in Encino. It was decided that we should shoot the actual exterior of the Hayvenhurst house to give the miniseries as much authenticity as possible. No cameras were allowed inside the house, however. For interiors we used another home in the neighborhood.

Jermaine's one act of playing producer involved our team of security guards. Jermaine insisted that they come from the Nation of Islam. Since our co-executive producer, Stan Margulies, was Jewish, I thought it would be an affront to him. Stan, to his credit, did his best to please everyone. The compromise was that half of the security guards would be from the Nation of Islam. They actually were extremely professional and well trained.

As soon as we returned to California, Jermaine had taken up his telephone vigil once again with Lea Bongo, who was still in exile in the far recesses of Africa. He felt my lack of interest in her painted me as a fair-weather friend and refused to take into consideration the pressures I was under from working on the miniseries. After his continual goading, though, I finally agreed to speak with her. I did have concern for Lea. I thought she had the potential to succeed and help her countrymen and that it was unfair she had been forced back to Africa by Madam.

When I spoke with Lea on the telephone, she said that she had her tuition money and that a living situation was the only thing preventing her from returning to L.A. In an effort to prove to Jermaine that I was capable of being a good and caring friend, I went to Katherine and asked her if she would mind if Lea moved in the guest room of Hayvenhurst for a few weeks until she could find a permanent place. I explained about her potential at UCLA and expressed my support for her education.

Katherine had no idea who Lea Bongo was but agreed that Lea could move in temporarily as a favor to me. She made some sort of comment about "too many hens in the henhouse," which at the time went right over my head. I reported back to Jermaine that Lea had gotten the green light for the guest room, and within the week the head count at Hayvenhurst had increased by one.

When Lea first arrived, Jermaine was spending most of his time with Bob Petrallia in New Jersey spinning his wheels on one project or another, so Lea fell under my jurisdiction. I had so little free time during this period that the most I could offer her was an invitation to come to the set of the miniseries and observe. I gave her open access to my trailer and the catering truck, and for the first few weeks she seemed to be content with that.

As anyone involved in filmmaking knows, boredom is your worst enemy on the set. Lighting and cameras have to be set up for every scene, and the downtime between takes is enormous. Lea found the entire experience tedious on a day-to-day basis and soon began to spend most of her days alone at Hayvenhurst.

Any day I expected her to return to UCLA for the summer quarter. Weeks turned into months and Lea had yet to begin school. When I would question her about it, she would always have a response ready. At first, it was that classes were getting ready to begin. That soon changed to a period where she was enrolling, followed by a request for money to buy books.

After Katherine donated $700 to the Lea book fund, I still didn't see any movement out the front door. Lea's next excuse was that she didn't have a way to get to UCLA from Encino. I personally couldn't understand the problem. I told Jermaine I was certain there was some sort of shuttle bus running to the campus. I even offered to give Lea a lift to some drop-off spot. The reaction I received was a bit over the top, even for Jermaine.

"You are the worst friend!" he shouted. He dismissed my suggestion as if I had expected Lea to walk the twenty miles. I do know that *I* was not about to drive this girl to school and pick her up. The way I saw it, any teenager with enough initiative should have been able to work this problem out on her own.

Jermaine's solution was to ask Katherine for the use of the BMW for Lea. It was a car that was used when other vehicles were being repaired, so it was available most of the time. I'm sure Katherine was surprised by the request, but could hardly deny Jermaine since the car was sitting unused in the garage. Getting Katherine's permission was still not enough for Jermaine. He continued to lambaste me for days to anyone who would listen to his version of how inconsiderate a friend I was to our houseguest. It was all part of a "get Margaret" campaign that had begun after Pittsburgh and continued through the remainder of our relationship.

Eventually, the subject of Lea's schooling passed, as each day she would disappear and return home in the evening, books and notebooks under her arm. Call it woman's intuition, but for some reason I had the feeling Lea wasn't attending UCLA. She never seemed to be doing homework or research or anything else that one would expect from a full-time student.

I called the UCLA admissions office to inquire if Lea Bongo was registered as a petroleum engineering and international business major. I was told no Lea Bongo was registered. I asked if she was enrolled in the UCLA Extension Program and was again told no. I tried not to think about it until, one day in August, I happened to see Lea while driving on Ventura Boulevard in the San Fernando Valley, smack in the middle of what should have been her school day. I told Jermaine. Not only was he not convinced Lea had been deceiving us, but he also didn't seem that interested even if it was true.

By this time the miniseries had finished shooting and had entered the editing and sound-mixing stages. My plate was full enough without having to worry about whatever it was Lea was doing. If no one else cared, why should I?

Had I been spending more time at Hayvenhurst, perhaps I would have seen what was apparent to everyone else. Lea was picking up Jermaine's clothes from the cleaners, wearing his shirts around the house, and jogging with him every morning. Lea was going with him to business meetings, typing his memos, and answering his phone. Her bedroom, located in the downstairs guest room, had turned into Jermaine's makeshift office and he was always in there with her. Sometimes a person needs to get smacked with a plank to get the point. This time it was Katherine who was going to deliver the blow.

She came to me one day after work and told me she didn't like what was going on between Lea and Jermaine. She didn't like it at all.

"It looks really bad, Margaret," she explained to me. "He's always in her bedroom. They're always together. The help is starting to talk, the security guards are laughing, and you're going around like you don't care."

I almost admitted to her that I didn't care. Actually, Lea was keeping him out of my hair so I could get on with the miniseries. But I told Katherine I would address the issue and a few days later confronted him. His reaction was vintage Jermaine.

"She's the only one helping me around here! You're never around," he said, pointing to all the time I was spending on what he called the "stupid little miniseries."

I could have stopped him midsentence to point out that the miniseries was the only source of income generated in the past two years. Instead, I allowed him to vent his anger. He told me that Lea was now his assistant and to mind my own business. When I brought up the subject of school, I was told that Lea was too smart for college, that her talents were being wasted there. She was going to be more than just a permanent houseguest.

The writing was on the wall.

11

Having their life story shown on television was an unsettling event for the Jacksons. As the various members of the family began to see dailies of the still unassembled miniseries, they would react with a plethora of wide-ranging emotions. Seeing the actors re-enact segments of their lives brought back all the love, the pain, the anticipation, the heartache, and, in several cases, the anguish as memories came flooding back.

During the tedious process of sound mixing and editing, I found myself working long days. One such day, Katherine had given me a ride to Universal Studios, where we were assembling the miniseries, and I invited her in to preview a particularly delicate scene. It depicted the moment when she intercepted a call between Joseph and his girlfriend, Cheryl Terrell. Katherine had heard the phone ringing on her way out to the car and had picked up an outside extension. Hearing Joseph and Cheryl speaking, she returned to the house to confront her husband. Angela Bassett and Lawrence Hilton-Jacobs threw themselves into their roles of Katherine and Joseph and were never better than in this particular scene.

At one point Angela picks up a jar of jelly beans and throws it at Lawrence, hitting him in the arm. I watched Katherine reliving the moment as she watched the screen. She was biting the inside of her cheek as she always did when she was angry, and she had her fists up to her chest. I heard her say, "Get 'im. Get 'im," as Angela attacked Lawrence in much the same way Katherine must have lashed out at Joseph twenty years before. She was smiling as she left the screening room.

Each of the brothers and sisters had his or her own story of life with Joseph—some sad, some angry. They would come to me, one by one, and share something they had hidden from the scriptwriter. Of all of them, Tito's was the most bitter. After watching some dailies, Tito came up to me with an uncharacteristic steely look in his eyes.

"You were very kind, Margaret," he told me. "The beatings, I mean. Joseph used to whip me with an ironing cord and then pour salt into the wounds." Tito seemed to have neither tears nor forgiveness, just memories that didn't go away.

Jackie, the athletic talent of the family, became emotional when watching scenes in which he was depicted playing baseball with his school team. I watched as tears came to his eyes and he began to sob. "Do you know that my father never came to watch me play ball?" he said. "My father never believed in me." His pain was hard to watch. I had hoped this miniseries would bring everyone together as a family. Instead, it just seemed to be evoking painful memories.

Away from work, life at Hayvenhurst had turned into a nasty TV soap opera, with much of the hostility directed at Joseph during his then infrequent visits to California. Despite his age and deteriorating physical condition, his children still lived in fear of their father because of his explosive temper and the collection of guns he kept upstairs underneath his bed and in his closet.

When Joseph got angry, his eyes would start to glaze over and his forehead would wrinkle. The transition was immediate and so identifiable that everyone who was able would run for cover.

He would charge up the stairs, and we never knew when he might bring down a loaded gun and start firing. It never seemed to matter how the argument started. It only mattered to Joseph that he won.

One afternoon Jackie and Joseph got into a shoving match. They fought quite a bit over women since Jackie, the most handsome brother, always had his pick of the lot and Joseph found that hard to deal with. Joseph wanted to have sex with everyone else's girlfriend or wife. This was hardly something new. Katherine told me she thought Joseph had slept with the wife of one of his brothers. Katherine's personal assistant, Amelia Paterson, physically stepped in between father and son to keep them from hurting each other. She knew better than anyone that a fight between Joseph and Jackie could easily turn deadly, just as it had for Marvin Gaye and his father. Amelia was a longtime friend of Katherine's and they loved each other like sisters. Because of that, she tolerated more from Joseph than any woman should ever have.

Amelia's office was in the back of the house, and frequently Jermaine, Jackie, and Randy would also use it to conduct business. One day it became the site of yet another family melodrama. Jackie and Randy were in a heated discussion with Jermaine over the way he was conducting family business. In the Jackson household, nothing stays quiet for long and, true to form, this discussion escalated to a fight at warp speed.

Hearing the argument, Joseph joined in, shouting his own insults. Then he got that familiar glazed look on his face and turned to leave. Amelia jumped to her feet to try to stop him, asking him where he was going. "I'm gonna get my tear gas gun and gas those boys outta there," the old man yelled. It was only because of Amelia's patience and abilities as a negotiator that Joseph didn't carry out his plan.

She had the respect of the entire family and her loyalty to them was never questioned. She would arrive at work and kid me that she was about to "put on her boots"; that was our inside joke about all the crap she had to wade through to deal with the Jacksons' business day after day. She told me that one time Jermaine walked up to her desk and exposed himself to her. To Amelia's everlasting credit, she remained unfazed. "Oh, Jermaine. Put that thing away. I've got work to do," she said, trying to dismiss the incident as a joke.

As the miniseries was winding down, we were counting the days until we would have a finished product to show the network. I knew in my heart that we had a winner and that the family was going to reap the benefits of the publicity both financially and emotionally. For another moment in time, they would once again feel like stars, and I wanted them to have that chance before making my own dash to freedom.

When I began to realize how many people would potentially be viewing the miniseries, I imagined other ways to capitalize on this one last gasp of fame for the Jacksons. Since no one had seen the family performing together since the *Victory* tour, I thought it would be the perfect time to try to reinvent the Jacksons once more with a single, pay-per-view concert. The advantages were obvious. Quick money, no long-term commitments, and Michael might just do it to make his family financially secure and get them off his back.

I asked Michael's manager, Sandy Gallin, for a meeting and was given ten minutes. Appearing at his office, I found I had been scheduled midway through a manicure appointment. As Sandy continued to get filed and buffed, I cut right to the chase. "There isn't any money for the grandchildren," I said. "And while I know this isn't Michael's personal problem, it is a family problem, which will make it Michael's problem eventually."

I proposed the concept of a single megaconcert, pay-per-view. I knew Michael was ready to tour with his *Dangerous* album and had already paid all the startup costs. I also knew that during the show he did a Jackson 5 medley backed by film footage of him and his brothers. I suggested the brothers could be incorporated live at this point.

To his credit and my gratitude, Sandy listened to every word I said and told me he would convey my concept to Michael and get back to me. It took him only twenty-four hours. "I told Michael about the meeting with you. It's a great idea, Margaret," he said, "but unfortunately, we've already done a deal with Michael to do a show on HBO."

He told me further that Michael's new deal with Sony Records didn't allow him to perform with anyone else. Even though I knew Michael would never have allowed himself to be boxed in like that with any record company, I politely said my thank-you's and chalked up the episode to experience. I had been getting a lot of that lately. Not a day would go by that I wasn't learning something new and, as a tenth-grade dropout, I was rather pleased with my accomplishments. Co-executive producer Suzanne de Passe also seemed pleased.

By this point in her career, Suzanne was already a Hollywood veteran and fast on her way to becoming the megaproducer she is today. She developed her reputation using her eye for talent, her strong sense of story, and her fundamental integrity, which I admired more than any of her other qualities. I was flattered when she complimented me on my work and said she would be happy to work with me again. To me it was the ultimate show of confidence, the vindication of my work ethic and an opportunity of a lifetime. I was not about to let it slip through my fingers.

I became partners with Suzanne's cousin Tony Jones, himself a Hollywood veteran. Tony was a producer at de Passe Entertainment and was a valuable executive on *The Jacksons: An American Dream*. He was attached to the project from the start and worked tirelessly. I was constantly amazed at how he could make the most difficult and complicated task look easy. He had a quick mind and an elephantine memory. We worked together well, so it seemed only natural to extend our relationship, and we started looking for more projects to produce. It helped bolster my self-confidence knowing that people well respected in the industry would value my input and abilities.

At home, however, Jermaine was on a nonstop campaign to turn me back into a stay-at-home housewife and mother. In addition to repeating his marriage proposal, he brought up the subject of another pregnancy. There was no way. Having given birth to two wonderful sons, I had no desire to head to the maternity ward again. My life was on a dramatic upswing. Working on the miniseries transformed me into a bird that had taken flight.

I was experiencing the rewards of being a productive woman and taking control of my own life. The last thing I was going to allow was for Jermaine to turn me back into a voiceless image in his shadow. Jermaine and I had been having personal problems, and our financial state was continuing to deteriorate. While Jermaine's money continued to disappear as quickly as it came in, I began to cover some of his debts with my producer's fees.

At this point Jermaine owed hundreds of thousands of dollars in back taxes, having failed to pay any capital gains tax on the sale of his Brentwood house or on the million or so he had gotten for the Arista Records deal. He owed a $200,000 balloon payment to Hazel as a result of their divorce settlement. His child support payments continued to pile up. He owed the settlement of our lease on the Beverly Glen house and the house we rented in Atlanta. He owed money to his lawyer, Joel Katz, his plastic surgeon, Raj Kanodia, his divorce attorney, and his business manager.

What compounded the problem was that Jermaine refused to stop spending. Because of expected tax liens, I had taken over control of the checkbook and our single credit card, but Jermaine would not think twice about sneaking the checkbook out of my purse and forging my name to buy things he wanted. He also memorized our credit card number and made purchases over the phone. And he still was trying to put together deals with Bob Petrallia and others of equally questionable ability. Every time Jermaine opened his mouth, it cost us another $5,000.

Despite all this, he was still pushing me to have another baby. He took his case to Katherine. "Speak to Margaret," he told her. She would bring up the subject with me, and each time my answer would be the same. "We can't afford it," I would tell her, explaining that while we were living in the Jackson family home and unable to stand on our own feet, having another child was out of the question.

"If I had waited until I could have afforded

children," she would say in return, "I wouldn't have any. You don't have children based on finances, Margaret. You do it out of love. If Jermaine wants another baby, you should have another baby."

When Mrs. Jackson said it, it sounded so logical, but what she didn't understand was that Jermaine didn't want another baby; he simply wanted me pregnant. He wanted to exercise control over my life. He wanted me unemployed and at home. That wasn't going to happen. Lea Bongo, however, seemed only too pleased to be at Jermaine's beck and call. The two began spending nearly every waking moment together. While they were not overly affectionate, they didn't make any secret of their friendship.

As autumn turned into winter, Joseph began to spend more time at Hayvenhurst. Although his stroke had softened his stride and weakened his ability to rage out of control, his lust for women continued undaunted. Throughout the years Joseph never seemed to be without some sort of paramour, and in late 1992 he was certainly no different. He had formed an alliance with yet another business partner, Hadje, an African from Senegal. One afternoon Hadje arrived for a meeting accompanied by a gorgeous black woman who was introduced to me as

Hadje's girlfriend. The introduction came with Joseph's own warning: "Don't tell Hadje's wife or his two kids."

The only one who didn't seem to know that the woman was his girlfriend was Hadje. He apparently had brought the young lady for Joseph's pleasure. Although she didn't stay long, at Hayvenhurst the walls have eyes, and Joseph and the woman were spotted kissing in the reflection of the swan pond.

Joseph was also rather blatant about his relationship with Terry Bingham, a blond, rather plain attorney who served as Joseph's lawyer on several occasions. Katherine and I would sit in the kitchen drinking hot chocolate and at midnight or 1 A.M. the telephone would ring. Without even acknowledging Katherine, Terry would ask to speak with Joseph.

"What's this woman doing calling my house at 12 o'clock at night?" Katherine would wail. "Is that normal for an attorney to call at 12 o'clock at night?" she'd ask, chewing on her cheek.

What Joseph's liaisons lacked in intrigue, they made up for in number. At the same time he was getting calls from Terry, he was also managing a Japanese singer named Mihoko. The woman was a frequent guest of Joseph's at his Las Vegas house, and Jerome Howard, Joseph's now former business manager, told me that he once walked into Joseph's room to get some papers and found the boss and the singer together in bed. This was the bed he shared with Katherine. After this story I wondered if Joseph had ever heard of a hotel.

At times Joseph's extracurricular activities got so bad that one of the Jackson brothers—who themselves were not always the souls of integrity—would confront these women. Even Jermaine took it upon himself to tell Terry Bingham to stay away from his father. Terry claimed that nothing was happening, but she made the interesting observation to Jermaine that Katherine was the one with all the power.

There had indeed been a change of guard at the Jackson house. Years before, when Katherine had joined Joseph in California, he was in total control, so much so that he didn't even want her to learn how to drive. Her job was in the home, scrubbing, cleaning, and taking care of the kids. Katherine was from the school that believed a woman's role in life was to give birth, nurture, and die. The concept of getting involved in business was foreign to her and Joseph never discussed the family business dealings with her. Only later, as the children matured, did Katherine come into her own. She's a savvy woman with wonderful natural instincts and possesses a certain logic that transcends education. As the children grew up and rebelled against Joseph's tyranny, they all turned to Katherine, their rock in the storm.

While Joseph had tremendous drive, he had no business sense. The children saw that repeatedly, even as kids. It was Joseph who had allowed them to sign off on their Motown contracts and royalties. And, as Joseph aged, his business practices became even more suspicious and plunged the family into lawsuit after lawsuit. Joseph's wheeling and dealing eventually turned into such a legal mess that he couldn't receive any direct income in his own name. Any money he was due went to Katherine. The woman who was told not to take driving lessons was now totally in the driver's seat, and it was a role she began to enjoy.

During the filming of the miniseries, Katherine came to me and told me Joseph needed $60,000 to invest in a new soft-drink company called Joe Cola. He was going to put his picture on the label and be as famous as Dr. Pepper, to hear him tell the tale. I was surprised she would even ask, although I kept my feelings to myself. Instead, I calmly explained that the money in the KJ Films' account was for use only on the miniseries. I stopped short of adding that if

Joseph ever realized he could get his fingers in the cash drawer, he'd move right in and set up housekeeping until it was drained as clean as his own accounts.

Katherine reported back to Joseph, who responded with one of his specialties, the evil eye. He gave me a look that said, "This is my family. This is my story. Who the hell do you think you are? You're lucky we even let you be involved."

As he was about to open his mouth to speak, I quickly rethought the entire scenario. Better to keep the peace than risk the entire miniseries. Before I realized it, I found myself saying, "How about $25,000?"

Joe's face lit up as if I had just shoved his big toe in a toaster. He took the money and seemed satisfied. None of us would have ever seen the money again had I not had it removed from his portion of a profit check months later. I was learning how to deal with him.

On another occasion Katherine requested a $20,000 "loan" for Bob Petrallia in New Jersey. Once again I went through my official line about the money being for the miniseries and any profit was earmarked for the family. She put her hand out and it stayed out. The money was eventually sent to Bob and, this time, with no one to charge it against, that loan became a forgotten memory.

On Sunday, November 15, 1992, ABC was scheduled to present Part One of *The Jacksons: An American Dream*. It was the culmination of four years of hard work, energy, and enthusiasm, and I couldn't wait until 8 P.M. to arrive.

If anyone else in the world had a miniseries made of their family life, there would have been balloons and limos everywhere and a fruit-and-cheese platter the size of Milwaukee. At the Jackson house, though, it was a slightly more intimate affair. Jackie made the trip to Hayvenhurst to join Katherine, Joseph, Jermaine, and me, plus the omnipresent Lea Bongo, in front of the set. None of the remainder of the family made an appearance, nor did they call when the telecast was over. We watched the first three hours in relative silence until the show ended. The final two hours aired three nights later, on Wednesday, November 18. It was a ratings smash and a critical success.

If I were expecting applause or even a pat on the back, I got neither. Lea Bongo said she liked it, as did Jackie, but Jermaine, Katherine, and Joseph took the show in stride without comment. But there was one thing no one needed to tell me: I had delivered on what I had set out to do.

The family had received more than $2 million in profits. The show was delivered on time and no lawsuit was ever connected with it. Unfortunately, what should have been one of the proudest days of my life was really the beginning of a nightmare—words and music by Jermaine Jackson.

12

"This is garbage!" Jermaine yelled as he sprinted past me toward the stairs, waving a copy of the *Hollywood Reporter*. He had just finished reading the announcement that ABC and de Passe Entertainment had optioned another property, to be produced by Tony Jones and me. It was a true-crime drama inspired by an article I had read in *Los Angeles* magazine.

"This is garbage!" Jermaine screamed again, throwing the newspaper into the fireplace in LaToya's old room.

Seeing my name in the industry newspaper pushed him over the edge. It didn't matter to him that after I had first seen the article, I had shared it with him and tried to get him involved in the project. He had laughed in my face, demeaning the entire effort as "some little TV movie."

What did matter was that suddenly there was no more denying the fact that I had moved to a different plateau in our relationship. Jermaine now saw me as a competitor rather than an ally. No longer could I possibly be expected to be the reliant, passive, adoring wife. As far as he was concerned, I was out of control and needed to be reined in quickly. Until that happened, he was no longer the master of his own game and he didn't like it, not one bit.

The fact of the matter was I had been working toward this moment from the second the end credits rolled. I had thrown myself into my new career and was excited about the prospect of working again under the de Passe Entertainment umbrella. After I dropped off Jeremy and Jourdynn at school, I would go to the de Passe office, leaving Jermaine and the ever-attentive Lea to their own mischief. Every day brought a new change in Jermaine's demeanor, the most pronounced being his abusive behavior toward our children. I believe in discipline, but it should be tempered with love and encouragement. If you reward children when they behave, most kids will do their best to be good. If you punish them too harshly for their mistakes, however, you risk the chance of making them fear rather than respect you.

Given the way the Jackson children were raised, I should not have been surprised when Jermaine started to spank Jeremy and Jourdynn with increased frequency and force. I begged him to stop, telling him that we weren't in Gary, Indiana, and that he wasn't his father.

To my surprise, Katherine didn't back me up. She sided with Jermaine, reciting the old chestnut "spare the rod, spoil the child." Complaining that I was spoiling our boys, Jermaine would take off his belt and beat Jeremy and Jourdynn. Both their nanny, Heidi, and I would try to stop him, until finally he would simply take the boys into a room and lock the door. We had to stand helplessly in the hallway hearing them scream. It was during those moments I felt the most powerless. I was determined to get them out.

About the same time, Michael Jackson had begun a three-month-long campaign to right his increasingly warped image. My reclusive brother-in-law, who previously had barely shown his unmasked face, suddenly was being seen everywhere.

He kicked off 1993 by singing "We Are the World" in Washington, D.C., at the presidential gala for Bill Clinton. Chelsea was positively unglued, Mom and Pop Clinton seemed pleased, and, as talent goes, this gala was one to remember. The Jackson family wasn't invited, so we watched it on TV. Everyone seemed almost bored by the hoopla. After all, we had heard the song so many times before.

Next up, Michael sang "Heal the World" at the Super Bowl, surrounded by children. With a cheering section of flash-card holders numbering about 100,000, he promoted his Heal the World inner-city charity. His performance, complete with pyrotechnics, lasers, and a 750-voice choir, was watched by more people in America than any other show ever. We were among them.

Michael then popped up at the NAACP Image Awards and the American Music Awards ceremonies, where he received an award from his buddy Elizabeth Taylor proclaiming him the "King of Pop, Rock, and Soul."

As impressive as all of those appearances were (and considering how few appearances he had recently made, they *were* impressive), Michael had one more card up his sleeve. It was the ultimate public relations dream: a ninety-minute Oprah Winfrey prime-time TV special to be conducted from Michael's own Neverland Ranch.

During the interview with Oprah, Michael spoke softly but directly, with no subjects off limits. No, he said, he didn't sleep in a hyperbaric chamber to extend his life. No, he hadn't tried to buy the bones of the Elephant Man. Yes, he loved being around the innocence of children. To viewers, the most amazing revelation during the special was the disclosure that he did not bleach his skin, which had become pale over the years. He talked about his skin disorder, vitiligo, which causes a loss of pigment and said that was why he wore so much makeup. The vitiligo came as no surprise to family members, who had known about it for years, but there was some surprise about Michael talking about the abuse he had suffered at the hands of his father.

The reaction toward Michael's interview was overwhelmingly positive. Just by being willing to answer the questions, Michael Jackson had been able to stop many of the rumors, distortions of truth, and innuendo. It served to bring leagues of fans back into his fold, and sales of his *Dangerous* album soared back into the Top 10.

Joseph and Katherine had watched the interview at Hayvenhurst and were stunned into silence by its candor. Although Joseph had expected to hear about the beatings Michael received at his hand during Michael's youth, that meant little compared to the one line that sent Joseph into an emotional tailspin. During the interview Michael said he feels nauseous every time he sees his father face-to-face.

Joseph's depression was quickly eased when he went on a tabloid show to respond to Michael's comment and said: "If Michael feels he has to regurgitate when he sees me," Joseph countered, "he's been regurgitating all the way to the bank for years." Joseph found a brand new Range Rover in the driveway as a gift from his son.

Lea Bongo, whom I had nicknamed "the African Queen," maintained her live-in status in the guest room despite my continuing pressure to give her the royal heave-ho. Having already begged Lea and pleaded with Katherine, I added an additional incentive. I wanted to give Lea $3,000 in cold cash to move. When I mentioned my idea to Katherine, she was not very happy about it. Her feeling was that Lea would go through the money and end up homeless and jobless.

I pushed Jermaine about the job issue, and he told me Lea didn't have a green card to work legally in the country. He had, however, come up with a plan that would allow Lea the opportunity to both stay and work in the United States. He wanted her to marry an American. He was not offering his own hand in marriage, which was, I must admit, the first thought that came to my mind. Instead, the husband-to-be was none other than Majestic the Magnificent. Majestic lived at Joseph and Katherine's house in Las Vegas in exchange for doing odd jobs around the place. One of the jobs included introducing Joseph to attractive women, a fact that Katherine acknowledged and accepted. At least with Majestic on the scene, Katherine could keep track of Joseph's philandering and business deals.

Majestic had a clever way of being able to straddle the fence, knowing exactly how much to tell Katherine and how much to do for Joseph. Now he was asked to go one step beyond his normal work as caretaker: marry Lea Bongo for a quick $4,000. It seemed somehow fitting that Las Vegas, where fortunes come and go in a flash, should provide the backdrop for this marriage of convenience. It took place in the same church where Joan Collins had tied the knot with her latest ex-husband.

Unfortunately, not even a wedding ring and a marriage certificate could shake the African Queen from her free room and board. No sooner had she become Mrs. Majestic than she was right back in action in the Hayvenhurst guest room. The only difference was now she could be legally paid for the privilege.

If Katherine was ineffective in getting Lea's

butt out the front door, Joseph was positively disruptive. He loved the fact that Lea was around because it kept things out of kilter, which worked to Joseph's advantage. Since I had effectively been replaced by Lea controlling Jermaine's business dealings, Joseph saw yet another opportunity to exercise some amount of control. As long as she got her room and board, Lea was everyone's friend. Every time I said, "Lea, get out," Joseph would shut me down by reminding me that it wasn't my house. "We want Lea here. She's staying," he'd say, just to see how upset he could get me. And the father of my children would be cheering him on.

It's hard to pinpoint exactly when Joseph's attitude became vicious. The first thing I noticed was his scowl. When I would speak, he'd respond with a scowl. Ask a question, another scowl. It was as if the child inside him had found someone he could finally annoy with his pettiness.

As the days went by, he increased his tactics, instructing the staff to inform him of my daily travels and log me carefully in and out of the property. In addition, he told one of the household employees not to help me and to act as if I were not even there. My mother and brother couldn't visit anymore. Joseph began referring to Lea as "Queen of the House" in my presence. He was beginning to play hardball, and Jermaine seemed to enjoy my discomfort.

Even with Jermaine's increasingly hostile attitude, I was convinced that our relationship wasn't at the root of the problem. I laid more of the blame on Jermaine's ruffled ego and lack of work. Then, surprisingly, he announced he had made a deal on his own. While I had been peddling projects around Hollywood, Jermaine had been trying to do the same. His goal was to become a bigtime producer and director. To that end, most of his projects were movie scripts. Unfortunately, they weren't particularly good ones. Not only didn't he have a bite, he didn't even have a nibble, until the day the development executives at NBC took a liking to a show called "Jackson Family Honors."

Jermaine's concept was simple enough. He would put on a two-hour prime-time special that would basically be a Jacksons awards show. The honorees: the Jackson Family. As crazy as it sounds, the idea was to have a Jacksons' show that patted the family on the back. That was the original concept NBC sent into development, with the ultimate sale hinging on an appearance by Michael, of course. At this point Michael had not even been approached with the idea.

The entire show sounded so narcissistic to me

that I almost couldn't keep a straight face when Jermaine was trumpeting his triumph. I asked him if he didn't think that perhaps it seemed a bit self-serving to give the first Jackson award to his father. He thought about it and agreed that I might have a valid point. When I suggested that Berry Gordy would be the far more likely (not to mention interesting) recipient, Jermaine said he would consider it.

I thought that when Jermaine opened his own production offices at Hollywood Center Studios that the illusion of being a producer—the position of being in control—would give him the self-confidence to come home feeling renewed, happy, and content in our relationship. I wanted things as peaceful as possible until I could get out. Instead, I saw each day disintegrate into verbal abuse and open hostility.

Jermaine wasn't the only one dishing it out in heavy doses. Across the country in New York, LaToya had made the news once more, this time as an abuse victim herself at the hands of husband Jack Gordon. The altercation happened in the wee hours of April 21, 1993, when Jack slugged LaToya in the face and lacerated her lip and right eye during an argument over her career. The argument apparently got out of hand. As LaToya raced to the front door of their highrise Manhattan apartment in an attempt to escape, Jack smashed a chair across her back, sending her crashing to the white marble floor.

LaToya called 911. When the police arrived, Jack was carted off to the nearest police precinct and charged with two counts of second-degree assault before being released on his own recognizance. LaToya was rushed to Lenox Hill Hospital for treatment of the cuts to her face and contusions to her legs, arms, and back.

News reporters alerted us to the attack with calls to the house as well as to Michael's Neverland compound. Michael telephoned LaToya and offered to fly her anywhere in the world to ensure her safety. Jermaine took the opportunity to reiterate his claim that Jack Gordon was a hustler and evil incarnate. Katherine dropped everything and headed immediately to New York with Amelia to see if she could talk some sense into LaToya at last. She wanted her daughter to come home.

None of the family's efforts made the slightest impression on Sister Black Sheep. In the aftermath of the attack, several points became clear. LaToya had had a kitchen knife in her hand, and Jack said she was going to use it to attack him. LaToya said she picked the knife up in self-defense. Also, Jack Gordon was being treated for inoperable cancer, and his behavior, according to

LaToya, was a reaction to the painkillers he was taking. In the end LaToya refused to press charges and refused to see Katherine, whose pleas for a reconciliation away from Jack Gordon fell on deaf ears. LaToya remained convinced that she needed Jack for guidance, and not even his physical abuse would sway her mind.

LaToya's older sister, Rebbie, remained silent during the entire ordeal, which surprised me. Rebbie had always impressed me as the Jackson daughter with the most compassion. It was Rebbie who had befriended Joh' Vonnie and it was Rebbie who was the first Jackson to extend herself to Alijandra after she became pregnant with Randy's first child.

Rebbie and her husband, Nathaniel Brown—a fellow Jehovah's Witness and hard-working driving school operator—had married when she was eighteen. After twenty-seven years of marriage, the only complaint they seemed to have was that money was tight. They would often come to Hayvenhurst, as much to raid the refrigerator as to visit. Whenever Katherine saw them coming, she would say, "Here come the vultures." Nathaniel and Rebbie not only would eat the food and drink the sodas, but would also even take bags of groceries home with them.

I recall an incident that occurred while

Jermaine and I were still living in the condo on Burton Way. Knowing Rebbie was always short on cash, I had thought of her when I got a call from a guy named Michael Mintz, who Jermaine had met years ago on a trip to Fiji. He owned a cosmetics company and wanted me to help him get to Janet. He thought she would be the perfect spokeswoman for his new line of cosmetics called Montage. Despite the fact that his company was respectable and previously had a deal with Shari Belafonte, I knew there was no way Janet would consider the deal for *any* amount of money.

Instead, I recommended that he talk to Rebbie. At that time Rebbie had a record deal at Motown. She had a terrific singing voice and a fabulous figure and would make the perfect image for Montage or any other cosmetic line. More important, I thought the price would be right. I told him if he was clever and approached things correctly, he might luck out and get the next Janet Jackson. The sound of image and dollars played a sonata in his mind. I even suggested he might want to consider a three-generation deal with Katherine, Rebbie, and Rebbie's two gorgeous daughters. But when Rebbie was approached, she made it clear that she wanted to do the deal herself.

Michael Mintz said he would fly to Los Angeles

to meet Rebbie, who was excited about the opportunity. Several weeks later we all met for lunch at the Beverly Hills Hotel. Rebbie brought her albums and photos for Michael to see. He loved Rebbie from the start and they made a deal that paid the eldest Jackson daughter $50,000 up front, with a promised six-figure back-end balloon payment.

By the time Jermaine and I had moved back into Hayvenhurst, the company eventually ended up going bankrupt and was unable to send Rebbie that final payment. She did, however, get her initial payment, as well as a gold watch for what amounted to a few hours' work on a photo shoot. I neither expected nor received anything for putting the two of them together, but I never even got a thank-you from Rebbie.

Meanwhile, brother Randy had begun an affair with model Paula Barbieri, which ended as quickly as it began. Paula would later become O. J. Simpson's girlfriend and get caught up in his murder trial. Having lost his condo on Wilshire, Randy moved into the Hayvenhurst house, settling into the upstairs den. He was still in the process of divorcing Eliza, who was now living in an apartment with their daughter, Stevanna. Despite their divorce proceedings, Randy would still occasionally sleep with Eliza, contributing to the ebb and flow of their love-hate relationship. During one of the "ebb" phases, Randy managed to get himself arrested. When Eliza sued Randy for divorce back in 1990, she had pressed civil charges against him for spousal abuse and he was placed on probation. In late 1991 he missed some of his counseling sessions, violating the terms of his parole. He was hauled back into court, where Katherine made an emotional plea for the judge not to throw her son in jail. Whatever she said must have worked because rather than go to the big house, Randy was committed for thirty days to the Pine Grove Mental Hospital for domestic violence counseling. While he did receive counseling, the thirty-day confinement wasn't exactly a punishment. He had his own private wing, and our cook took him special meals every day, complete with an appropriate wine. And members of the family were allowed unlimited visitation. Even so, Randy learned a valuable lesson.

Somehow the stay in the mental hospital seemed perfectly in character with a romance and marriage that was a complete melodrama from the start. Randy had met Eliza in a nightclub, and they were married before a justice of the peace, both dressed in sweat clothes. After she filed for divorce, but before he moved out of his Wilshire Boulevard condo, Eliza would block Randy's car and picket in front of the building holding a sign accusing him of being a "Deadbeat Dad" for failing to pay child support.

But Eliza and Stevanna weren't Randy's only concern. His on-again, off-again girlfriend, Alijandra Loaiza, and their daughter, Genevieve, had left the country and were living in South America with Alijandra's mother. It was hardly a vacation for them, though. Alijandra's mother was a convicted cocaine dealer who had served time in a California state penitentiary. After she was paroled she fled the country and went back to her native Colombia. After Genevieve was born, I stayed in touch with Alijandra and, during the course of one of our conversations, Alijandra told me she had had several abortions, all paid for by Randy. I wasn't surprised. Randy always said he wouldn't be like the rest of his brothers and have a bunch of babies all over the place. I guess he figured if he couldn't stop them before conception, he would stop them after. When Alijandra found out she was pregnant with Genevieve, however, she didn't tell Randy about the baby until long after she felt it was too late to stop the pregnancy.

With two children by two different women, Randy wasn't eager to have another baby. He hadn't counted on the fertility of Alijandra Loaiza. She became pregnant again by Randy, who was then still married to Eliza. Knowing his feelings about having more children, she left the country for Colombia.

Randy didn't discover that there was a Randy Jr. until several weeks after Alijandra left town. He flew down to retrieve Alijandra and their daughter, but had to leave Baby Randy behind while the intricacies of his dual citizenship were worked out. Several weeks later, with paperwork in hand, Alijandra and Randy returned to Colombia to be reunited with their infant son. The trip would turn out to be one that the Jacksons would never forget.

According to Randy, while driving alone he was stopped at a roadblock by the ELN rebel army, a group that raised capital by kidnapping foreigners and holding them for ransom. Demanding his passport, the rebels took one look at the name Jackson and saw dollar signs. Randy sidestepped the issue of ransom by telling them that he was a Rastafarian evangelist with no money of his own. After the guerrillas threatened to chop off his fingers if he was lying, they tore off his shirt, tied him to a tree and left him for dead.

By the time Randy freed himself and made his

way to the U.S. embassy, he was covered with insect bites and suffering from exposure. The incident proved to be more than a horrible tale to tell when Randy returned home, leaving Alijandra and the children in Colombia. It provided Alijandra with some added ammunition of her own. Now thoroughly convinced that her children were in danger of being kidnapped by guerrillas and held for ransom, she telephoned Katherine with her suspicions, asking to be brought to the safety of America. Since Randy had refused to marry Alijandra on several occasions and didn't like the idea of her being around, he did his best to discourage any outpouring of compassion for the woman and her children.

Yet none of us could imagine letting the Jackson babies grow up in South America, especially me. We could see what it had already done to Genevieve, who was then three and couldn't speak a word of English. I went to Katherine and opened the door on the discussion to allow them to come and stay at the Jackson compound.

It wasn't a hard sell. Katherine sent Alijandra plane tickets and days later welcomed her new family with open arms, directing that the gym be converted into another bedroom for the newest Jacksons. With that, Alijandra moved into Hayvenhurst and set off a string of reactions that would impact us all.

The arrival of Alijandra, Genevieve, and Randy Jr. at Hayvenhurst was a blessing for me. More than just a young, fun-loving woman, Alijandra was someone with whom I could talk about anything. I felt we shared a kindred spirit. Ever since our paths had inexplicably crossed in that boutique in Beverly Hills, our lives seemed to be linked. I welcomed the arrival of my friend.

She was an ally against the absurdity of Lea Bongo and Jermaine. Despite Jermaine's continuing insistence that the two of them were nothing but good friends, I was getting bombarded with rumors that their relationship was sexual. Most of them were coming from within the family.

I was speaking with Randy and Alijandra one afternoon when Jackie arrived at the house unexpectedly. He seemed withdrawn and upset and I soon learned why. He and Randy told me that they knew for a fact that Jermaine was sleeping with Lea and that it had been going on for some time. Jackie said he had seen Jermaine and Lea in Jermaine's car at Balboa Park one morning. No news there. They went there every morning to jog.

"The windows were steamy," Jackie continued.

He didn't have to say more.

Randy backed up his brother's story and added that the cook had told him he had seen the two of them coming out of a motel on Ventura Boulevard on his way to work. Leave it to Jermaine to pick the motel where the cook was staying temporarily while his quarters were being remodeled.

I didn't rage or cry. In fact, I felt relief. It was as if some sort of sign had been sent down to me that it was all right that I wanted to be out of my situation. This was just one more reason. I didn't need any more.

There is a certain embarrassment that goes along with knowing your husband is sleeping with a member of your own household. If that person is attractive and dynamic and has a body that would make grown men weep, you might not like it, but you might understand the situation. Lea, however, was overweight and unattractive; even the security guards had trouble keeping a straight face when she walked by. She apparently had something the Jackson men loved, though, because it wasn't long before Jermaine wasn't the only recipient of her favors.

I was in the kitchen with the cook, Katherine, and Alijandra one evening when Joseph came walking in from the direction of Lea's room. As he walked past me, I noticed a condom hanging out of his pocket. When he saw that I had spotted it, he jammed it quickly in his pocket and kept moving. Who's to say whether he did it on purpose? Still, the idea of both the grandfather and the father of my children sleeping with the same woman disgusted me.

Randy was up to his old tricks, too. While the mother of two of his three children was sleeping on a bed in the Jackson's converted gym, Randy was going off to have sex with his almost ex-wife. He and Eliza were suing each other for divorce but that didn't seem to matter. When he wasn't with Eliza, he was with Alijandra, each woman fully knowing about the other. Eliza would call the house and scream at Katherine because the Jacksons were housing the woman who broke up her marriage to Randy. Alijandra would complain that Randy was always sneaking off to sleep with the woman who hated him so much that she was suing him for divorce. When the two women would get on the phone together, it sounded like a cat fight.

It wasn't any calmer on the business front. As I became more comfortable in my role as a producer, I would spend more and more time away from Hayvenhurst. Away from home, I had a sense of self-respect and a feeling that I was able to make a difference—two things that disappeared immediately inside the Jackson compound. Jermaine was aware that he was losing me and that the "other man" in this case was my work. He would think nothing of calling Tony Jones and yelling at him over the telephone. Tony, who had known and watched out for Jermaine during the Jackson 5 days, found himself again playing nursemaid to the man.

Jermaine would question Tony about my income, my business, and my projects. And he would do his best to lace his comments with guilt. "How could you do this?" he'd bellow to Tony. "We've been friends for so many years."

It was a line Tony was prepared for. He'd once told me that I was outgrowing the Jacksons. At the time I didn't understand him. Despite Tony's assurances that Jermaine was powerless to prevent my involvement with de Passe Entertainment, it didn't stop Jermaine from trying.

When demands didn't work, Jermaine tried threats, telling Tony that he would see to it that the Jackson family would sever its ties with him and Suzanne, and that a relationship that spanned twenty years would be ruined. It was exactly the kind of threat Tony Jones knew how to handle. He simply ignored it, and it went away like the hollow fabrication it was.

I suppose it was inevitable that the day would come when I would walk in on Jermaine having one of those telephone conversations. Hearing what he was saying to Tony, I was furious. I couldn't imagine what Tony was thinking, but I certainly knew what I was. When I told Jermaine to stop calling my office and badgering my friends, he threw down the telephone. I grabbed it quickly to apologize to Tony, who did not deserve this kind of treatment. As I was saying I was sorry, I felt Jermaine's hand slam into my face.

There was a moment—that second between impact and pain—that I stopped breathing. I was still holding the phone, and I heard myself screaming into it. Tony was yelling my name on the other end of the line. I don't know if I was more scared or more angry at what had happened. I told Tony I'd call him back and hung up the receiver.

Turning to face Jermaine, I saw something that broke my heart. My two sons had witnessed the attack and were staring at both of us.

"Why did you hit Mommy?" Jeremy asked in a voice softer than normal.

"Because Mommy was being bad," Jermaine answered and left the room.

I ran over and hugged my boys and told them everything was going to be all right. As the words came out of my mouth, I wondered, silently, how in God's name I was ever going to get out of Hayvenhurst so I could make those words come true.

I went racing down the hall to find Katherine, who was in her bedroom. "I don't know what has gone on here in the past, but Jermaine just hit me in front of the boys. He told them that he did it because 'Mommy was being bad'! I'll tell you one thing, it's never going to happen again," I said in a voice so controlled that I gave her no choice but to agree.

Unfortunately, it did happen again, and again, and again. The reason was immaterial, the outcome always the same. Jermaine would lose control of the situation and had only physical force to place himself back in charge. He would twist my arm behind me, push me around the room, and then toss me down like a rag. He needed no other reason than the frustration of a relationship that had collapsed.

Joseph would exacerbate the problem by sneering or scowling whenever he walked past me. Joseph felt he had me figuratively pinned in a corner and was delighted by his ability to make me squirm. I hated it and wanted Jermaine to stop his father out of common decency. Jermaine refused, just as Jermaine usually refused to do anything that would put him at odds with Joseph.

At one point I accused him of acting like a "woosie." Jermaine charged across the room and hit me so hard he knocked me through a closet door. Pinning me to the ground, he grabbed my crotch. "Now who's the pussy, Margaret?" he said, his face contorted with anger. He had misunderstood what I had said, but there was no misunderstanding that he was out of control. I spoke very calmly, trying to reassure him that I had said "woosie," adding that I really didn't even mean to say that word. I apologized, cajoled, and tried flattery. The tension slowly drained from his body and he stood up. He looked like a warrior who had been victorious in battle as he strutted out of the room. It would have been almost funny if it wasn't so terrifying.

Again, I went to Katherine and told her what had happened. Again, she told me a story of her own. She said one time Joseph had come after her, intent on hitting her. She said she picked up a glass ashtray and threw it directly at her husband. The edge of the ashtray slashed his arm. "Joseph took one look at the blood, and from that point on, he never, ever messed with me," said Katherine.

She then took my hands in hers and said, "Margaret, if you ever have a problem with Jermaine again, just draw blood once, and you'll never have another problem again."

I understood what Katherine was telling me, but her "fight fire with fire" philosophy didn't exactly inspire me. I just wanted to leave Hayvenhurst and this dysfunctional family behind. I was looking for something, anything, that would allow me a steady income so I could take the boys and get out. Then Jermaine's and my business manager, Howard Grossman, introduced me to Anita Camarata.

Anita was a talent manager, and Howard thought she and I might work well together. I arranged to meet Anita over lunch in the Sunset Plaza area of West Hollywood. Sniffing a business deal in the making, Jermaine insisted on tagging along. After showing absolutely no interest before, Jermaine suddenly became interested in my projects.

I managed to throw him off the scent long enough to have this first meeting alone with Anita. She ran a company called Eclipse Management, which represented various artists. Our first joint management deal was an agreement to work with a group of gorgeous, talented women called Ebony Vibe, similar to the singing group En Vogue. It was a long shot, but I had to get away from Jermaine and his family.

I never thought of myself as a victim. It was not a role I could or would play. From the first time Jermaine raised his hand to me, he was history, as far as I was concerned. But I now understand what makes some women stay in abusive situations. There are a lot of psychological reasons, but for me it was plain economics. When you have two children, no personal money, no job, and only dreams, it is hard to walk. There is also that little voice in the back of your head that whispers, "Maybe, if your husband begins to feel better about himself, things will change and be like they used to be."

Do not listen to that little voice. Once someone starts hurting you, there is no going back to the way things used to be. Things probably weren't so good anyway, the way they used to be. My mind had known this for a long time and the rest of me was finally coming around. I was determined to have enough confidence in myself to get out and make it on my own. If I could afford some of the niceties I'd become accustomed to, so much the better. I deserved them. I earned them.

In addition to spending days at de Passe, I began spending a portion of my nights at Eclipse, but although my new alliance gave me another possible avenue of escape, it served to give Jermaine another target for harassment. I had only been working with Anita for a few weeks when I discovered that Jermaine had shown up in front of her building with Jeremy and Jourdynn, screaming to the doorman to allow them inside. I wasn't even there at the time, having gone out for a business meeting.

"These children need their mother," Jermaine was saying. "She should be home cooking their dinner and she's here working. What kind of mother would do that?"

I'm not certain what the doorman told him. It would have been perfect if he had replied that the world was full of working mothers trying to earn a living to pay bills while their husbands played at being a businessman with a chunky little girl from Africa. Somehow I doubt that happened.

What I know for a fact is that ten days later Jermaine made another surprise visit, this time to the recording studio where Ebony Vibe was listening to some new tracks. Anita and I were trying to work with one of the hottest writer-producers in the business, nineteen-year-old Vincent Herbert. We had taken him out to dinner and then brought him by the studio afterward to hear the group. We were hoping he would like what he heard and would agree to produce something for them.

As I walked to my car afterward with Gina, one of the women in Ebony Vibe, I noticed her eyes widen to the size of two casaba melons. I turned to see Jermaine racing toward us from across the street.

My first thought was of the semiautomatic he always carried in the back of his jeans. He had once been deputized by the sheriff in New Orleans, which he thought gave him the right to carry an unregistered gun anywhere. I moved away from Gina, hoping to keep her out of whatever was going to happen. Jermaine seemed to be in a wild rage as he rushed up, grabbed me by the arm, and threw me to the ground.

"Call the police!" I shouted to Gina. She stood glued to the spot. "Now!" I added.

I had no clue what Jermaine would do, especially when I noticed the friend at his side, an off-duty Los Angeles policeman. Like a lot of celebrities, Jermaine had friends on the police force.

Gina ran into the studio and brought half the people in the building out to help me. By that time I had struggled to my feet, pleading with Jermaine to stop scaring everyone, including me. He grabbed the car keys out of my hand and started screaming, "You wouldn't have this car if it weren't for me. The only reason you know anything is because of me."

He jumped into my Mercedes and tried to start the car as everyone stood there watching him. By then my fear was turning to anger and I had enough composure to move toward his policeman friend and tell him he had better warn Jermaine not to take my car. The Mercedes was in my name and I would not have hesitated to have Jermaine Jackson tossed in jail for grand theft auto.

The car engine roared. Jermaine threw my car into reverse, hit the accelerator, and, in his fury, smashed the car into a tree. He was totally and completely out of control. I knew it and the off-duty police officer knew it. As the policeman tried his best to calm him down, Jermaine got out of the car and now directed his attack at my new partner, Anita.

"You promised me! You promised me! You promised me that if I let her work with you, she wouldn't be out at night at recording studios! This is crazy!" he sputtered.

Jermaine had lost what little grip on reality he had. To say that he "let" me work was absurd; to think that he could control my business hours was equally ridiculous. Coaxed by his policeman friend, he left the parking lot as quickly as he had arrived. I looked around and saw Anita, the Ebony Vibe members, and the record producer I was trying to impress all looking at me in stunned silence. I didn't know what to say.

Jermaine retaliated for having to back away from that encounter by flaunting his dominance over me in front of Jeremy and Jourdynn. Not content with just screaming at me, he brought the children in to watch the display.

"Your mother is a whore," he shouted to them. "All she cares about is money. She doesn't care about us being a family anymore."

How odd to hear those words spewing from Jermaine's lips, and to think back over the years and remember my thoughts when I first crossed

Hayvenhurst's threshold. The Jacksons were going to be the family I never had. To hear Jermaine say that family meant nothing to me reinforced how distorted his perception of our problem really was.

I knew I needed help. I later suggested to Jermaine that we talk to a marriage counselor. To me, professional help was our final chance to salvage what remained of a very damaged relationship. I got Jermaine to agree, and together we made our first appointment with a psychologist, unsure of what direction the therapy would take.

At the session Jermaine explained to the therapist his feelings about my working. I explained my feelings about our financial crisis. Jermaine said I wouldn't have sex with him. I revealed the presence of a houseguest named Lea Bongo. The therapist looked at us both as if we were truly out of our minds. She said that the first step toward healing was to remove Lea from the picture. That was all Jermaine had to hear. He went on the defensive with the counselor.

"I don't like the fact that Margaret's working and managing other people. Take care of that problem, then I'll see to it that Lea gets out of the house. And that's the deal," Jermaine said.

The therapy session ended and Jermaine never

went back. I continued going on my own for several more sessions, but until Jermaine understood that his refusal to release control of me was at the root of our problems, there was no point in trying to salvage any part of our relationship.

I told Katherine what the therapist had said, and she told me that the answer to the problem was simple: give up my work. "Why?" I asked. "So that I can be like Enid? So that I can be like DeeDee? So that I can be like you? I'm not giving it up. If Jermaine loved me he would respect me as a person and encourage me in what I choose to do."

Katherine didn't get it. That wasn't the way she saw things. There was nothing more to say.

Rather than improving, the situation with Lea actually began escalating after the therapy session. As if to prove a point, Jermaine flaunted Lea in front of me like a possession as often as possible. He increasingly resorted to physical violence to get my attention. Whenever he didn't direct it at me personally, he took his agression out on the house. Walls were punched, doors were knocked down, glasses were broken.

I was frightened and told Katherine I was worried that something horrible would happen. The poor woman, by this time, had been diagnosed with high blood pressure. I knew if I stayed around much longer I would be in the same shape. My options were limited, however, and of the few at my disposal, Katherine was the best.

I wanted Lea out. I felt it was bad for my children to see their father carrying on with another woman while we were all living in the same house. Every time I spoke to Katherine about Lea she would promise to do something, but she did nothing except look the other direction. I was becoming desperate to get enough money together so the children and I could leave.

Out of some foolish sense of duty, I took one of my payments as a producer on the miniseries and gave Hazel several thousand dollars to cover Jermaine's debt in unpaid child support. I also used $20,000 to pay off a bank loan for Jermaine, took care of the $10,000 bill from a storage company that was threatening to sell Jermaine's musical equipment, and made a $25,000 tax payment Jermaine owed to the IRS for a tour in Japan he had processed under my name.

That done, I seized every opportunity to advance my knowledge and get a leg up on the business ladder. And I continued to network around Hollywood, believing in my own abilities. On the evening of July 4, 1993, I had been out to dinner with a group of friends and returned to

Hayvenhurst about 9:30 that night. I went up to our room and found Jermaine had taken all my clothes out of the closet. He had ripped up many of them and tossed the rest around the room. It looked like a scene from a sick movie, complete with a message scrawled on the mirror with my reddest shade of lipstick. It read: GET OUT BITCH! in big, bold letters. I'm not sure how long I stared at those words. It had all come down to this.

I knew I had to make my move.

14

The devastating message Jermaine had left on the mirror in our room was burned into my brain. I remember my hands shaking as I dialed my mother's number. This would be one time I would not turn to Katherine. I needed my own mother, and my brother, Willie, as well. I called them both and asked them to come and stay with me for the night. I was afraid of what else might happen that evening at Hayvenhurst. My mother and Willie came and offered comfort and sympathy, but I knew I would never feel safe in that house again.

The guards, the cameras, the walkie-talkies, the heat sensors, the laser beams—all the security was directed outside, not inside. Nothing was going to protect me in that house. If any of the

Jacksons knew what Jermaine had done, they would look to me for reasons. I would take the fall; somehow it would become my fault. They played by the house rules, and they made the rules up as they went along.

Jermaine wasn't around that night, but he returned the next morning. He didn't apologize. Instead, he blamed me for aggravating the situation to the point where he "had to do something."

I said nothing. I knew the direction our relationship was taking. I was fighting a war with a stranger and the only question now was when the next round would begin. I didn't have long to wait.

In mid-July 1993, Jermaine and I went to a country/western club in Santa Monica called Denim and Diamonds, where Suzanne de Passe was having a birthday party. Everyone was having a good time until Jermaine, fueled by Long Island iced teas, decided I was flirting with my handsome hairdresser, Nick Chavez.

Jermaine grabbed me by the back of my hair and pulled me through the crowd and out into the parking lot. I was screaming for him to stop but he wasn't listening. He slammed me against a car. I managed to break away, darting between cars like Wonder Woman in some Hollywood thriller. Only this wasn't a movie, and Jermaine wasn't acting.

I finally made it to our car, jumped in, and locked the doors. As Jermaine ran toward me, I started the engine and drove away. I called the house on the car phone and Joseph answered. I told him that his son was acting crazy, that he had been drinking, and that Joseph had better come to pick him up. It all turned out to be unnecessary. When I pulled into the driveway at Hayvenhurst, Jermaine was right behind me in a taxi. Joseph was outside, watching us pull in. As I got out of the car and headed toward the house he approached me menacingly.

"What did you do to my son?" he demanded.

I wanted to take my fist and shove it right down his throat. I had wanted to do that a lot lately, but as usual I held my temper and tried to maintain my dignity.

"Ask your son," I said, and kept walking. Joseph probably taunted Jermaine for not having better control of his wife.

The scenario would repeat itself in various locations with various players, but each time the result would be the same: insane behavior and general craziness. It was giving me a headache. Migraines, actually. I wasn't sleeping, my appetite was sporadic, and my emotions began to vacillate between feelings of determination and despair. My confidante through this particular time of crisis was Alijandra. On the one hand, she was a wonderful listener and certainly understood what it was like to live inside the fishbowl called Hayvenhurst. On the other hand, she was a hot-blooded Latina who was always eager to settle things physically.

"How can you *not* want to beat up Lea?" she asked continually. "She's sleeping with Jermaine right in this house. If it were me, I'd . . ." She would make a fist and say something in Spanish.

Physical violence was not my style, but I was not above a little abject begging. I went to Katherine to plead with her to front me some money so that I could move out with my kids. I thought she'd be happy to have all the fighting and violence come to an end.

Her response would always be the same: "Stay, Margaret. You're overreacting. We'll work this out for the sake of the children." Then she'd say, "I don't have any money," almost as an afterthought.

I found it hard to believe she thought I was overreacting, considering all the broken objects around the house. But then again, she hadn't seen Jermaine when that look of rage came over him, and she hadn't seen Lea goading him on.

One afternoon I confronted Lea. I was standing at the top of the stairs as she walked through the foyer. I didn't mince words. I wanted her to know she was no longer welcome around me, my children, or Jermaine. I shouted for her to leave. Get out. Then I added the words *voodoo witch*. Okay, I admit the name calling was pretty immature, but I felt I was at the end of my rope.

Jermaine and Katherine came out of their rooms just as Lea took off her shoes and rushed up the stairs to attack me. She pulled my hair, knocked me down to the ground, and tried to hit me in the face with her shoe. Jermaine grabbed her arms and pulled her off of me. As he did, I looked up and saw that Jeremy and Jourdynn were in the foyer. Humiliated at having my sons see me involved in a fistfight, I grabbed my car keys and raced from the house. I jumped into my Mercedes and sped out the driveway past the surprised security guards.

It wasn't until I hit the nearest main street that I realized what I had done. I was in my car while my kids were still at the house with Lea and Jermaine. I made an illegal U-turn and returned to Hayvenhurst. When I entered the house, I heard voices coming from the guest room where Lea stayed. I walked into that room and, in front of Lea, Katherine, and Jermaine, made my stand.

"I am not the type of person who gets into fistfights, Lea. Don't you ever hit me in front of my children again," I said to her.

Lea wasted no time in responding. She almost knocked Katherine over trying to get at me. I fought back as best I could, blocking her fists as she swung wildly at me. Once again, Jermaine pulled her off of me and I went running up the stairs to my room. I thought Lea would be history after that exhibition, but I hadn't counted on the Jacksons' quirky brand of logic. "I didn't know you could fight like that," Jermaine said to me, obviously pleased to be living with a duke-'em-out kind of gal.

Neither Katherine nor Jermaine seemed to realize this sort of display might be damaging to my children. Only the combatant Alijandra told me, in her broken English, that I should leave. "Oh, Margaret," she said, "Jermaine is crazy. He love you but he don't know how to show it right. You should go quick before something really bad happens here."

I certainly agreed with her, but I still had a barren bank account and two children to support.

At Hayvenhurst, as in most of Hollywood, it didn't take long before rumors started spreading. Perhaps it was the gossip among the security guards and the cooks that convinced Jermaine I was serious about leaving. The concept brought out the worst in him and he started threatening me with the one thing he knew would frighten me. "You leave here and you'll never get custody of the children," Jermaine said. "Someone with your past, no judge in his right mind would allow you to have the children," he said.

I was losing my grip and my sense of humor was history. I wondered whether Jermaine was right. Sometimes idle threats carry more of a punch than real ones do. He knew that if I thought he might be right, I would never have budged from Hayvenhurst.

Curiously, as our relationship continued to disintegrate, so did his interest in our children. Jermaine was spending more and more time away from home. He traveled to Switzerland on mystery trips and often was in New Jersey with Bob Petrallia working on the "Jackson Family Honors" show. Jermaine had hired Gary Smith as the executive producer of the special, which was a smart move because Gary is well regarded in the entertainment industry.

Word started filtering out that the show would be broadcast from Atlantic City and would be produced in association with the Casino Association of New Jersey Inc. (CANJI). CANJI was promising to put up $6 million for the production, which was expected to generate $1.3 million in ticket sales from various casinos in the area. That would cover Gary Smith's costs, and additional money from the network license fees would be donated to charity.

I found it strange that Jermaine and his family would consider giving money to charity when they couldn't even afford to send my kids to the dentist. I remember thinking to myself, *Charity begins at home*.

The periods when Jermaine was out of town became my periods of peace and quiet. As soon as he returned, I could depend on instant drama and continuing chaos. He now became violent without any provocation, and breaking, busting, and crashing sounds accompanied every argument.

I was frightened because Katherine was traveling and was away from the house for days at a time. With Katherine gone, Jermaine and Joseph became lords of the manor, and the person these macho men usually chose to bully was me. Because I knew the slightest thing could set either of them off, I tried to stay invisible. On several occasions I wasn't quite invisible enough.

One evening Jermaine came at me for some reason and I rushed down the hall toward Katherine's room, not knowing she wasn't there. I banged on the door, pleading with her to help me. As Jermaine headed toward me, the door opened and there stood Joseph in the doorway.

"What?!" he snapped.

"It's Jermaine! He's after me again," I said frantically.

"So what? You ain't dead yet," he retorted, and slammed the door shut.

That particular night Jermaine didn't attack me, but I knew it would only be days before some other perceived slight would set him off again.

On May 5, 1993, Jermaine and I were having a discussion about friends, which was a joke since I had no real friends outside of Tony Jones, Anita Camarata, and Randy's girlfriend, Alijandra. That didn't matter to Jermaine. He wanted to make a point.

"The only reason anyone is your friend, Margaret, is to get to the Jackson family," Jermaine reasoned. "They don't want to be with you, they want to be near us."

Given the three friends I could call my own, the comment was laughable. Tony Jones had known Jermaine since he was fourteen years old and had had more of Jermaine than he needed in two lifetimes. Anita was terrified of Jermaine and did her best to keep as far away from him as possible. And Alijandra was in love with his brother and had already been involved with Randy before Jermaine and I had even met. Usually Jermaine was at a loss for words, so if he had a point to make he made it physically. One time he threatened to tear my head off and the look in his eyes told me he might try.

With Katherine gone, I wasn't going to take any chances. I told Jermaine I was calling the police and immediately picked up the phone and called 911. I told the 911 operator that my life was in danger just as Jermaine pulled the phone out of the wall.

Within minutes the police had traced the call and were at the front gate. There was a standoff as the security guards refused to let them inside the compound. Even after Joseph came out and assured them everything was all right, the policemen, to their credit, refused to leave until they had spoken with me. I could see their blinking lights from the bedroom as Jermaine shouted that I had embarrassed the entire family. I didn't look at it quite the same way. I wanted him to know that I wasn't going to tolerate his abuse any longer and I wanted some help on my side.

When I saw the police enter the house, tears flooded my eyes. I met with them in the downstairs trophy room. They were total strangers, but I was so grateful to have someone sane listen to me that I couldn't stop crying. I thanked them again and again for coming. I was asked if I had been attacked by Jermaine. I said I hadn't been—not this time. I told them about all the threats in the past, though, and they listened patiently to everything I said. I know the policemen were just doing their job, but they did it with such compassion that I will always be grateful to them.

They suggested I get out of the house. I wanted to leap into their car and let them take me away, anywhere. Of course, I couldn't. I had Jourdynn and Jeremy to think about. It was bad enough that my two sons knew there were police in the house. It was traumatic for them, but I had to make my point. I had to let Jermaine know there was a line he could no longer cross. There was now an official police report of the incident and Jermaine now knew that I would not hesitate to pick up the telephone and call them again.

Although I had had a positive experience with law officials, the best known member of the Jackson family would not fare as well.

On the evening of August 23, 1993, NBC-TV in Los Angeles televised a special report. Police had entered Michael Jackson's Neverland compound and Century City condominium, armed with search warrants. The news report said that it was part of an ongoing investigation of Michael. The charge: child molestation.

15

The concept that Michael Jackson could molest a child is absurd to me. There is nothing I have ever seen in this man during all the years I've known him that would ever suggest he would be capable of carrying out such a heinous act. I didn't believe a word of it and neither did anyone else in the family. As jealous as the brothers may have been of their superstar brother, they couldn't believe it. It absolutely couldn't be so.

It was no secret to any of us that Michael surrounded himself with children. They were his playmates in a world of money-hungry opportunists, the one group of individuals who were not out for anything other than a happy time. At least until now. Ever since Michael had bought the

Neverland Ranch, he had made a habit of entertaining children, including both physically and mentally challenged kids. He loved their willingness to treat him like someone other than a superstar. He loved their honesty, their innocence, their laughter.

As various groups of children came and went through his life, there were some that got repeat invites to the ranch, among them the boy whose father now accused Michael of molesting his son. Michael had invited the child to see him perform in concert and took his mother and sister with them to Monte Carlo to watch him accept the World Music Award for Entertainer of the Decade. Executive producer Gary Pudney, who had arranged for Michael's participation in the program, provided suites for the entire Jackson entourage at the famed Hotel de Paris. A private dinner was scheduled at the palace of Prince Rainier, but after Michael learned that his guests weren't included on the invitation list, he canceled his appearance.

The boy sat with Michael during the awards program, and both were dressed in identical black outfits and red armbands. The show was broadcast around the world. There was never any attempt made to keep the boy's identity a secret. Michael was just offering the child a fabulous, once-in-a-lifetime opportunity.

Returning home after stops at Euro Disney in Paris and Walt Disney World in Orlando, Florida, Michael continued to prepare for the long-anticipated world tour of his *Dangerous* album. The first hint that anything was out of the ordinary came via a telephone call from the boy's father, a Beverly Hills dentist and would-be screenwriter. The man demanded a meeting with Michael concerning his son. The family would later learn that the dentist had been peddling a script he had written to Michael's representatives, who made the mistake of stringing the man along. Michael's people alleged that the father attempted to extort money from them in exchange for his silence about what he believed was misconduct on the part of Michael toward his son.

Michael dismissed the demands as extortion and left the country to begin his *Dangerous* tour in Bangkok. As things unfolded, he should have taken the man's threats more seriously. The fact that the American press was having a field day was kept from my brother-in-law by a tight net of advisers who closed him off from outside contact.

Upon hearing the news, Katherine tried in vain to reach her son to tell him what he must have already known: that she supported him completely. One person who did penetrate the security net was Elizabeth Taylor. Michael had telephoned her soon after the story broke and asked her to come and stand by his side. It was a familiar role for Elizabeth, who also had stood by her friend Rock Hudson as he told the world he was dying of AIDS. She wanted nothing other than to help a friend in need.

I can't say the same for Jermaine, who seized the opportunity to swing the spotlight characteristically onto himself. With journalists now camped outside our front gate, Jermaine decided to capitalize on the moment. He walked out to the gate and held an impromptu press conference in support of Michael. It seemed each day provided still another opportunity for Jermaine or Joseph to speak to the press. When Jermaine spoke he usually was holding Jeremy or Jourdynn or both. Finally, I got fed up with the whole circus and told him I was pulling the plug. If he wanted to speak to the press, that was his business, but I told him to leave our children out of it.

He took advantage of the situation to announce the "Jackson Family Honors" TV special. Jermaine told the press that he thought Michael was "the victim of a cruel and obvious attempt to take advantage of his fame." Was Jermaine doing anything less? Jermaine announced that all the Jacksons would participate in the family honors show, even though he knew Michael had shown no interest in the project and had certainly not agreed to do it.

LaToya appeared on the "Today" show, saying she knew Michael loved to entertain "lots of little boys" in his room at Hayvenhurst, which was outrageous since the "little boys" he entertained were his own favorite nephews, Taj, Terrell, and T.J. They frequently visited their uncle Michael and spent hours playing video games and watching movies with him in his room.

Meanwhile, Jermaine, Katherine, and Joseph flew to Taiwan where Michael was now touring. To all the world, the gesture was to show support for Michael. What the press didn't know was that in his pocket Jermaine had a letter of intent for the "Jackson Family Honors" show, which he was determined to get Michael to sign. He finally succeeded, but Katherine was furious that Jermaine and Joseph hounded Michael into signing it at a time when Michael was under a doctor's care for exhaustion and being fed intravenously.

The fallout from the molestation scandal was devastating to Jermaine and his show. The entertainers who had committed to the program began to drop out by the handful, and no one was stepping forward to take their places. The pressure was on Gary Smith to produce a program that looked unproducible, and once again

Jermaine blamed Michael in private for his problems while continuing to support him in public. The tension between Jermaine and me was hardly helped by the pressure put upon him as his special began to disintegrate. The saving grace was that he was still spending much of his time outside of the house.

Everyone in the household was running on emotional empty when a document started to make the rounds at Hayvenhurst. A security guard brought me a piece of paper at 10 P.M. one night and told me to sign it. He stood there and watched as I scanned what appeared to be a legal document. On it was attached a note that read: "Michael's and Janet's offices have asked me to have everyone who lives in this house sign this agreement and I hope you understand. . . . Love, Katherine."

It was a confidentiality agreement, which had obviously been prepared with the house staff in mind. It referred to the signer as an employee and said that he or she was not to take any pictures of the family or discuss anything that went on inside the house with anyone outside of the house. I laughed out loud, thinking it was some sort of mistake, and handed the agreement back to the guard.

When Jermaine arrived home later that night,

I wasn't prepared for another showdown. "Sign it, Margaret. Now," he said, throwing the agreement in my face.

It had gotten to the point where Jermaine's outbursts were so melodramatic, so larger than life, that I had to fight to keep from laughing. I picked up the paper and calmly handed it back to him, telling him he was never going to get me to sign anything under duress.

The next day the problem was resolved after my attorney faxed a copy of the agreement to Michael's office and I received a swift and unequivocal apology. "Sorry, Margaret. That wasn't meant for you," I was told.

On September 14, the earth fell in on Michael Jackson, and all of us were caught in the aftermath. A lawsuit was filed at Santa Monica Courthouse by the boy's father. The story was on every newscast, on every tabloid show, in every newspaper, in every scandal sheet. The gates outside the property were canvassed day and night by journalists, cameramen, and photographers. Helicopters watched us from above; paparazzi tracked us on the road.

Doing normal business became nearly impossible and I spent most of my days inside watching the media circus. I had a momentary diversion when a television producer friend of mine in

New York City called and asked me if I could arrange an interview with Heidi Fleiss.

The Hollywood madam's story had broken several weeks before Michael's and she was still hot news to the networks. She promised to try to get a producer credit for me if I could arrange an interview. Given my contacts from my wild and free drug days, I thought it was possible. I placed a call to Victoria Sellers, a former acquaintance. Victoria and I weren't close, but she was tight with Heidi, and I knew a few friends of Victoria's stepdad, Lou Adler, so we had enough common ground to give me entrée. Victoria agreed to put the two of us in touch and moments later, I was cross-connected to the Hollywood Madam herself.

Despite all her problems, we shared a good laugh over what the press would make of it if she paid a visit to the Jackson compound. She did eventually speak with my producer friend but ultimately declined the interview. It seemed her terms were too tough: She wanted the interview to follow the Super Bowl and she wanted to advertise her line of lingerie. Say what you will about Heidi Fleiss; she's a businesswoman.

By the time Halloween was upon us, the entire molestation mess had become a feeding frenzy for teams of attorneys on both sides. Each side was playing its case out in the press, but fan support for Michael seemed to be holding firm. At this point he was continuing his world tour and had moved from Moscow to Tel Aviv to Gstaad, Switzerland, where he camped out with a few of his child friends in Elizabeth Taylor's chalet in open defiance of his advisers. After a few more days, he would travel to Mexico City, where an abscessed tooth would add to his problems.

To get everyone's mind off the media hoopla, I decided to throw a Halloween party for the kids, a party that would end up creating a hassle for Randy. I rented a giant bouncing balloon, Hazel brought piñatas, and my mother helped decorate the place with spiderwebs and goblins around every corner. Hayvenhurst, which singer James DeBarge once called "the House of Fear," made the perfect Halloween hangout. (James had been married to Janet Jackson briefly in the 1980s and had lived with her at Hayvenhurst. Once, when he was despondent over something or high on drugs, James had climbed up on the roof and threatened suicide. Joseph came out of the house, took one look at his son-in-law, and told him to jump.)

If Katherine hadn't been out of town on tour with Janet, the Halloween party would have gone perfectly. With Katherine gone, though, and Jermaine in Switzerland, Joseph was in charge and pushing his weight around. The call he placed to Randy's estranged wife, Eliza, was done out of pure malice. He knew it would create a problem for his youngest son. What he didn't realize was that it would also create a problem for himself.

When Randy discovered that Eliza was at the front gate with their daughter, Stevanna, he confronted Joseph and the two of them got into a scuffle. Then Joseph headed toward his bedroom. Fearing Joseph was going for his guns, Randy grabbed onto his father's shirt, ripping the material and pulling the elder Jackson down a flight of stairs.

By the time I arrived on the scene, a security guard was pointing a gun at Randy, attempting to follow Joseph's instructions to throw him off the property. What I hadn't realized was that Joseph had told the security guard that Randy was drunk as an excuse to give him the boot. Obviously, there was no liquor at a children's party, but then no one has ever said that the Jacksons' security guards were hired for their intellect.

Randy eventually left, totally humiliated. Later that night he telephoned in tears. "Can you believe how my father treated me?" he said, sobbing. There was little that I could say in the way of comfort except to tell him that I would update Jermaine when the two of us spoke and ask him to speak to Joseph about his behavior.

The more I thought about what happened, the angrier I got. I picked up the phone and called Jermaine to vent my frustration.

"I can't take it anymore. I really can't," I told Jermaine when I reached him at his cousin Elizabeth's house. "The combination of Lea, your father, and the circus of press at the front gate is too much. I would rather starve than deal with this one more day."

I could almost hear Jermaine's ego puffing up over the long-distance line. "I'm a Jackson. I'm not moving out. I have to live where there's security. Just get that out of your head. That's not happening."

When I told him about Joseph's behavior, Jermaine focused the attention away from the craziness of his father and blamed Randy. The more we talked, the more excited Jermaine became. He was sputtering things like "Fuck Randy" and "Randy can't control his women."

I went over the edge. "You know what, Jermaine?" I said. "You just don't get it. You're never going to get it. I don't want to be with you anymore. You disgust me. Your family disgusts me. You're a loser, you're a has-been. I haven't wanted to sleep with you for two years. I've been putting up with this bullshit because I've been trying to make it work for my kids' sake. Well, it's over, and as far as I'm concerned, I don't care if I never see you again." I slammed down the phone.

I had held in my anger, my frustration, for so long that the words spewed forth in a torrent. It didn't matter that they weren't beautifully constructed words or powerful prose. I said what I meant and I felt good about it. I went to sleep that night with a smile on my face.

The next morning, however, I was no longer smiling. There was a strange undercurrent in the household. Katherine was looking at me as if I were the devil. I couldn't figure out why until Lea told me that Jermaine had had a heart attack in Switzerland after I had spoken to him the previous night.

I didn't believe it for a minute. It was too convenient, too well timed, and quite frankly, I'm simply not that lucky. I knew Jermaine too well to buy into his sympathy routine. The real story turned out to be something more like heart palpitations brought on by anxiety. A heart attack it was not.

When Jermaine returned to the United States,

he was certainly no worse for wear. He vacillated wildly between telling me how much he loved me and smothering me with attention, and tossing me around and cursing the ground I walked on. Threats were commonplace.

"If you ever leave me, Margaret," Jermaine sneered, "I'm gonna rip those titties of yours right out of your chest and put them on 'Entertainment Tonight.'" He would prance around the room, holding out his hands as if he were holding my breasts and humming the "Entertainment Tonight" theme.

Alijandra became my relief valve as the pressure began to build. Because the security guards had the ability to listen into any room through the intercom system, Alijandra and I would creep into my bathroom, turn on all the water, smoke cigarettes, and talk. She wasn't a professional psychologist, but she had the most important quality: She was there. The more we talked, the more hopeless I knew the situation was, and the more frightened for my safety I became.

Every day seemed to bring new drama, none more unexpected than the surprise incident that occurred on November 8, 1993, while the family was in Phoenix, Arizona, for the funeral of Joseph's father, Bud. Without warning, the gates were opened and sixteen undercover police officers stormed the Hayvenhurst house, armed with a search warrant. They went to work sifting through drawers, closets, and cupboards, but concentrated their search in Michael's room. A locksmith picked the lock to gain access to his area of the house. The men proceeded to tear through his belongings, which Katherine had carefully preserved exactly as Michael had left them. The security guards called her in Phoenix and she rushed back in time to find the house in disarray.

The search was in full swing when I returned from picking up the kids at school to discover the invasion army. They went through my closets and even Jeremy and Jourdynn's toys. Katherine was in a rage. The police, nevertheless, went about their business and carted away four dozen boxes of family possessions.

Michael heard about the search while he was in Mexico. He reacted with what the media described as a breakdown that sent Elizabeth Taylor back to his side. Michael completed the last of his performances in Mexico and was jetted out of the country to England, where staff at the famous Charter Nightingale Clinic took charge.

As far as the world knew, Michael Jackson had simply dropped out of sight.

On November 12, we learned that Michael had

canceled the remainder of his *Dangerous* tour because of an addiction to painkillers. The media went crazy and redoubled their efforts to keep a twenty-four-hour vigil at the front gates of Hayvenhurst. We were assaulted with questions and cameras as we came and went, and from the children's bedroom window, Jeremy and Jourdynn had a perfect view of the proceedings. I wanted them out of this environment but still couldn't figure out how to get the money. Then one day I ran into an old friend, Mario, in a parking lot. He invited me to lunch the following afternoon. The next day, he must have seen all the anger, frustration, and fear etched in my face. "Margaret, you look horrible," he said, and asked if there was anything he could do.

By the time I had finished explaining my situation, the plates had been cleared and the iced tea drained and refilled several times. Mario offered what I needed most: cash and some good advice. He told me not to worry so much and to take things one day at a time. Then he wrote me a check.

First, I had to find a place to rent and was lucky enough to find a reasonably priced three-bedroom apartment with hardwood floors and high ceilings on a quiet, tree-lined street. Knowing that it would be quite a change from

Hayvenhurst, I took my two boys to preview their new home. If they were disappointed by its size or location, they didn't show it. Instead, they were excited and full of energy.

Jermaine adjusted with less enthusiasm. I told him I would be moving out of Hayvenhurst on December 11, and as that date grew closer, he actually mellowed into a kinder, gentler soul than he had been in the past several years. Despite everything we had been through, there was a part of me that wanted to reach out and console him. His pain was extreme and obvious, and witnessing it wrenched my own soul and sensibilities. Jermaine had some wonderful qualities that I will never forget. Unfortunately, in the last years of our relationship, they were hidden with increasing frequency under a thick blanket of anger. Perhaps he was scared of what he was becoming. I knew for sure that I didn't want to be near it.

When the moving van arrived as planned on December 11, 1993, the movers packed up my clothes, a few TVs, a couple of beds, my armoire, and the kids' toys. It should have been a simple move, but as I walked down the hallway of the Jackson compound for the last time, I realized there was nothing simple about moving on.

Jermaine and I shared a long, final embrace in

the driveway. There were no good-byes, only tears. Tears for the times we would never share, and for the opportunities lost to recapture a love that at one time was real and beautiful.

There were no winners in this drama. His failure was my failure. What was ending for him was also ending for me, and we both knew there was no turning back.

As I got into my car and drove away, I looked in the rearview mirror and saw the gates closing behind me. I couldn't help but recall what DeeDee had said years before: "Remember, Margaret, when those gates close, they stay closed forever."

16

On the day I left Hayvenhurst, Michael
Jackson reentered the United States to
face the allegations against him. Given
the legal entanglements that the case presented,
Michael decided to strike a settlement with the
boy and his father rather than spend endless
years in litigation. Every member of the family
was disappointed in Michael's decision to settle
the case, because we all knew he was innocent.

At my new home I sorted through clothes and
boxes as I started to set up house. With only the
few things I had brought with me, the apartment
was nearly empty. I didn't have much, not even
kitchen utensils, but I did have a lot of help from
Heidi, Jeremy and Jourdynn's nanny. She was
more than a help. She'd become a lifesaver who

had lived through all the emotional turbulence of our lives at Hayvenhurst. During our last months there, Jermaine had tried to fire Heidi on an almost daily basis. He knew her presence allowed me to continue to put my career together, and he wanted her out.

At one point she was so terrified of Jermaine that she had taken to sleeping under her bed in the hope that she could fake him into thinking she was gone. She wasn't completely successful. I would walk into her bedroom and see her empty bed but hear loud snoring coming from somewhere in the room. I'd look under the bed and there she was, curled up and sleeping on the floor.

Her nighttime ritual didn't change much when we moved. She was still sleeping on the floor, but this time it was because of a shortage of beds. Despite the fact that she had been unpaid for weeks, she stayed and remained loyal to the kids and me, and for that I will be eternally grateful.

Jermaine began calling the day after I moved, accusing me of leaving just when the Jacksons needed a show of solidarity. I felt badly about that, but I knew it was just his way of trying to make me feel guilty. I also knew he had to vent his anger, so I listened without responding. The more tolerant I tried to be, the more frustrated he seemed to become.

For me, the move had a calming effect. I didn't miss having a cook, a maid, a pool, or a screening room at my disposal, which was hard for Jermaine to understand. He couldn't fathom how I could be happy to leave all that behind.

I felt what I was getting in return was more than an even trade-off. For the first time in several years, the migraines I had suffered—headaches so painful I would just lie in the dark and cry—had disappeared completely. I saw my boys laughing and happy instead of worrying about a police invasion or the press camped out at the gate. My brother and my mother helped me find household items. Slowly my apartment began to feel like home.

For Christmas, Hazel had given the kids a basketball hoop and backboard and, not having a backyard or much indoor furniture, I allowed them to set it up in the living room. It was more like a gym than your average Beverly Hills household, but it was home for us and we loved it.

Jermaine continued calling every day, several times a day. He was an emotional person, and given the tension he was under after I left, I thought he might be in danger of having a total breakdown. One moment he was my best friend; the next, my worst enemy. He cried, he screamed, he even threatened. Regardless of how hostile or abusive his language became, I reminded myself to remain calm and be pleasant. I didn't want to provoke him and have him storm over to my apartment. I thought I would treat him like an adult, show him respect, and hope for the best.

While I continued to pursue my career, I approached Jermaine about child support. Even though I knew he didn't like discussing the subject, I worked it into every conversation. At first his answer was a simple no. "I don't have anything, and you'll get it when I get it," he said.

When I would ask him how he expected his children to eat, he told me I should have thought of that before I moved out. "Send the kids back. They won't starve here," he replied.

It was a circular argument that was not about to go anywhere. The thought of finding a family law attorney came to mind, and I knew that eventually I would have to cross that bridge. At the moment, however, my thoughts were on a more immediate source of cash.

Polygram Films still owed KJ Films Inc. a final $2 million payment for the miniseries. It was being held in trust until Michael signed off on an agreement stating that he had no preexisting contracts with any other company for his life rights. Michael had had the agreements for over a year but had yet to sign.

In addition to money owed me as a producer on the project, there were many outstanding payments to others, among them executive producers Suzanne de Passe and Stan Margulies, the William Morris Agency, the Loeb and Loeb law firm, business manager Howard Grossman, and the Gordy Company for sync rights, plus some lingering bills, including payment for repairing damage to a swimming pool we had used on location.

I happened to bump into John Branca, Michael's attorney, at a school function. My son Jourdynn and one of John's children were in the same class. This was a golden opportunity to bring up the outstanding unsigned agreement. I explained that Michael's failure to sign on the dotted line was holding up a $2 million payment to KJ Films. It was money that was owed to a lot of people, including me. The fact that Jermaine and I had split didn't surprise him. Neither did the knowledge that I could make good use of any funds due me. He promised that he would look into it. "These child molestation things they say about Michael," John said. "It's amazing what people will do for money."

I was happy to hear John supported Michael

and knew as I did that Michael was totally innocent. I also knew that I could trust him. About a
week later, the law firm of Loeb and Loeb received Michael's signature on the required document. Armed with the agreement, Loeb and Loeb
sent it to Polygram and received a check made
out to KJ Films Inc. for a little under $2 million
in return.

Since I was still chairman of the board and
chief executive officer of KJ Films and had always handled payments during the course of
the miniseries, the attorneys at Loeb and Loeb
notified me of the arrival of the final payment. It
was quite a moment when they handed me the
check. I, Margaret Maldonado Jackson, the person the family was turning its back on, was
holding a check for nearly $2 million. I would
have given anything to see Joseph's face when
he found out.

I wanted to pay off everyone who was still
owed money and then disperse the profits to all
of the Jackson ex-wives who were owed child
support by members of the family. It was a fan-
tasy I was forced to dismiss, but it bothered me
that the Jacksons thought they could thumb
their noses at the laws that protect wives and
children from deadbeat dads.

I negotiated Loeb and Loeb's fee down to fifty

cents on the dollar in an effort to give more profit back to the family. For their part, it had been so long since the miniseries aired that they were happy to receive whatever they could get. I also paid our outstanding contractual obligations to Stan Margulies and Suzanne de Passe, the Gordy Company, Howard Grossman's accounting firm, and the William Morris Agency. And I had a check cut for my own final producer's fee of $60,000.

The bank made out the checks, and I personally drove around town and delivered them. With each delivery came a warning to cash the checks immediately and almost no one questioned my meaning. Unfortunately, the Gordy Company held on to the check and when they finally deposited it, the account had been closed. To this day, as far as I know, they've yet to be paid.

After everyone had been paid, there was $934,916.47 left for the family to split eleven ways. Jermaine's share would have been a little less than $85,000. At this point Jermaine still owed me more than $80,00 in funds that I had advanced him over the past year, including the child support money to Hazel, the repayment of Jermaine's bank loan, the fees I paid on the storage locker, and the Japan tour taxes. Since I didn't want to take all his money, I left him nearly

$14,000 and kept $71,000 to cover at least a portion of what he owed me. Had I left all of Jermaine's money in the bank with the expectation that he would use it to repay me, I knew I wouldn't stand a chance of seeing it. Not in this lifetime.

I realize now that I put Howard Grossman in an uncomfortable position by asking him to call Katherine and tell her that the family's money was sitting in the bank. I was leaving for a while. I was terrified of Jermaine and knew that he wouldn't be happy that he had "repaid" me for his outstanding loans. What I didn't expect was Katherine's reaction. She was outraged that I had gotten that check and paid the outstanding debts due on the miniseries. According to Katherine, since I had left the family, I no longer had a responsibility to the show. She didn't realize or wouldn't admit that I was still an officer of the corporation, and my responsibilities as a producer hadn't ended when I left Jermaine.

While I was still out of town, I called our attorney at Loeb and Loeb, who had been informed that Katherine was anything but pleased. The lawyer said that Katherine felt the firm had acted irresponsibly in giving me the check, to which Loeb and Loeb countered that I was still the chairman of the corporation and was the legally responsible party to handle the matter. When I returned home, Howard Grossman told me that the Jacksons were accusing him of conspiring with me against them, which was totally untrue.

The next telephone call came from the bank. They had frozen my personal bank account. I had unwisely opened my own account at the same bank I used to deposit the KJ Films check. They had access to both accounts and froze both.

Katherine had gone to the bank with her attorney Terry Bingham, the very same attorney she had earlier complained would call Joseph at midnight or 1 A.M. They informed the bank that I was unauthorized to open an account in KJ Films' name or write any checks from the account.

Since it was a large amount of money and involved the notorious Jackson family, the bank got nervous and put everyone's money on hold until they could sort out who had the real power in this play. They told me that the money would be held in the accounts for twenty-four hours and if nothing had been resolved by that point, they would leave the final disposition up to the courts.

The bank had me on a speakerphone, and in the background I heard Katherine ask me, "Why did you do that, Margaret? Why did you take the money?"

I told her that I didn't "take" anything. I paid out funds that were contractually owed. This wasn't an arbitrary decision; this was a legal obligation. Ignoring my comment, she shifted the subject and suggested I had taken money that belonged to Jermaine.

"We lived with you, Katherine," I responded, wanting the bank officers to hear. "You know that I paid Jermaine's child support to Hazel. You know that I personally paid off his bank loan and storage fees. You know that I paid his back taxes. You're the first person who would know because you heard me complain every day about it. And you also heard him say that he would pay me back."

She said that Jermaine would have paid me when he could. She suggested that he always took care of his children. I shouldn't have had to remind Katherine that if it weren't for me, Hazel wouldn't have gotten any of the money she was paid during the eight years I was with Jermaine. But remind her I did. I knew too much to fall for the Jackson line that had worked so well on others in the past.

I offered a compromise. I would put Jermaine's money into an account in which both her signature and my signature would be required to pay any bills. She would therefore be able to see that every penny was going to support Jeremy and Jourdynn. It was logical; it was fair. Katherine refused.

There was dead silence. It was the financial version of a Mexican standoff. True, I would be out $140,000, but Katherine and the Jacksons would be out almost $1 million if the funds were tied up in litigation. Finally, Katherine said, "Let her keep the money."

The bank released the funds and we were required to sign paperwork that indicated that the matter was settled. The truth was that while I got to keep my fair share and Katherine got to dispense the remaining profits to the family, the issue was far from over.

The calls started the second I returned from a trip to Aspen.

"Give me my money." It was Jermaine demanding that I return the funds I used to repay his loans. "Give me my money now, Margaret."

I wasn't in the mood to be dictated to by this man, but once again I tolerated it for the moment, explaining to him that I had left nearly $14,000 in the account for him. Jermaine was outraged, claiming that Katherine hadn't given him a dime. The calls became more and more heated—different verse, same chorus: "Give me my money!"

Within days Jermaine began to change his approach, asking me if I could send Hazel $5,000 for him. The thought that I had left Jermaine, left the Jackson family, and was still expected to pay child support to Hazel was ridiculous. I was sorry to hear that Hazel wasn't getting paid now that I was gone, but it was no longer my concern. It was, however, the very reason I had left Jermaine some money in the account and I told him exactly that. If Hazel had called me directly, I would have tried to get her some money. Perhaps not the whole $5,000, but something if she was in a pinch. As it turned out, Hazel never brought it up, even though we were in contact. My kids visited Jaimy at Hazel's house on a regular basis and enjoyed a close friendship.

Over the years I had gained a lot of respect for Hazel and the way she raised her children, and I felt the same way about DeeDee, who was an outstanding mother. DeeDee and I saw each other infrequently after she was dropped by the family, but I knew she never really got over the loss of Tito. I wish now that I had had more time to talk with DeeDee, particularly in light of what happened on the morning of August 27, 1994.

Before dawn, Delores "DeeDee" Jackson, age

thirty-nine, was found dead in the pool of her boyfriend Donald Bohana's house in Ladera Heights. The shock of DeeDee's death was compounded by the coroner's report, which indicated that her body had numerous cuts and bruises to her lips, tongue, ear, and head. According to Deputy Medical Examiner David M. Posey, the cause of death was "asphyxia, due to or as a consequence of drowning, alcohol intake, and blunt-force traumatic injuries."

I showed up at DeeDee's funeral at the invitation of her son Taj. After everyone was seated, the Jacksons and their entourage made a grand entrance and walked to the front of the assembled crowd. The eulogy suggested she was a cherished member of the Jackson family. No mention was made of the fact that every one of the Jacksons, save Michael, had had nothing to do with her for the six years since she divorced Tito. Only Michael offered DeeDee a financial helping hand, primarily in support of her three sons.

As I write this, DeeDee's death remains an unsolved case with the Los Angeles Police Department. In late August 1995, however, her sons filed a wrongful death suit asking unspecified damages. In the suit it was charged that Bohana was enraged because she wouldn't bail him out of bankruptcy and that he spent four hours beating her before he held her head underwater, killing her. The suit was filed in the U.S. District Court just before the statute of limitations expired.

DeeDee's death made me cherish my relationship with Hazel all the more. I encouraged my children's friendship with her youngest son, who is their age. One evening when the kids were visiting Hazel and Jaimy, I drove over to her house to pick them up. The iron gates at the front of the property were open. As I pulled my Range Rover up to the front door, Jermaine suddenly jumped out from behind another car and started to scream at me to get out of my car.

I've done some crazy things in my life, but getting out of my car at that point wasn't going to be one of them. Checking that the doors were locked, I yelled through the closed windows for him to leave me alone.

"I want my money, Margaret. Damn it. I want my money, now!"

Knowing this was not the best time or place to have a discussion, I started to back my car down the driveway. As I continued to back up, and Jermaine saw that he couldn't stop me, he threw himself onto the hood of my car as if he were in a Sylvester Stallone film. The scene was as pathetic as it was ridiculous. I would have been laughing at the sight of him hanging on like some inept stuntman if it weren't for the fact that he was wearing a huge silver belt buckle that was digging its way into the paint on my hood.

I reached the bottom of the driveway and pulled into the street just as Jermaine began pounding on my windshield, screaming incoherently. The thought that he would kill me on the spot flashed through my mind. Knowing that I had to do something to get him off my hood, I floored the gas pedal and drove several feet up the block before suddenly slamming on the brakes. This maneuver always seemed to work in movies. On that night, though, it was less than successful.

Sensing that it was a standoff, Jermaine jumped off of my hood and karate-kicked a huge dent in the driver's side door. As I watched all this happen, the thought flashed through my mind that this jerk was not only refusing to talk about paying child support to help his kids eat, but now he was actually costing me money. The repair bill kept getting larger and larger with each passing second as he kicked and banged and punched my car in frustration.

I floored the gas pedal again in an effort to escape and drove like a maniac down the street, running through stop signs and red lights. I wanted to stop and call the police but was afraid that Jermaine might be right behind me with his gun. When I neared a friend's home, I rushed inside to use the phone.

The first call I made was to Hazel to confirm that Jeremy and Jourdynn were okay. To my horror, Lea Bongo picked up the telephone. Lea Bongo, the African Queen, was in Hazel's house with my children! The instinct of a mother to protect her children is one of the strongest in the human psyche. Mine was raging.

"What do you want?" she snapped into the receiver.

Trying not to sound scared, I told her that I wanted my children.

"Well, you're not getting them, bitch," came the reply. And with that she slammed down the phone.

My next call was to the police, who agreed to meet me at Hazel's house. I waited on the corner of her street until the police officers arrived. When I followed them up to the house, they told me I would have to wait in the police car while they questioned Jermaine. They searched me and asked about my right to custody of the children. I suddenly began to feel like a criminal. I was the injured party, yet to the police there are two sides to every story. So far they had only heard one. While I waited in the police car, they disappeared into Hazel's house.

Hazel was inside with her three children, Jaimy, Jermaine Jr., and Autumn; Jermaine was inside with my two kids, Jeremy and Jourdynn, along with the omnipresent Lea Bongo. An hour went by before anyone emerged. When the door finally opened, the kids were led out of the house by the police. Jeremy and Jourdynn were in tears.

"Mommy, why did you try to kill Daddy?" Jourdynn asked, sobbing.

I denied that accusation as gently as I could, but with little effect. My children were convinced that Jermaine had jumped on the hood to save himself as I stepped on the gas to run him down. They were too young to realize that I had been backing away from him, not driving toward him. As I continued to try to calm down my children, one of the policemen shoved a clipboard in my hand and told me to sign the police report of the incident. It was dark, I was tired, and my children thought their mother was one step below a murderer. I signed the report without checking it and went home.

After putting Jeremy and Jourdynn to bed and warning them against the dangers of violent behavior, I noticed there was a message on my answering machine. It wasn't easy for me to hear the hate-filled words of Jermaine's teenage daughter, Autumn.

There is a certain point in life when one begins to question whether all the positive energy that's put out in the world is ever reciprocated with anything other than a slap in the face. I had reached that point. I had never treated Autumn with anything but respect. Even more astounding was that there had been no call from Hazel. She knew better than anyone what was going on between Jermaine and me, yet she allowed me to walk right into that setup. It was cruel and it was dangerous. The following day Hazel did call to tell me she had tried to head me off before I arrived at the house.

When I thought about what had happened, I realized Jermaine's actions had less of an impact on me than what Autumn had said. She was so young and there was such hatred in her voice. I looked at the police report and began to understand why all the children were so upset. Jermaine had told the police that he had wanted to talk with me, and I had responded by using my car as a lethal weapon. The entire concept was ridiculous. If I had wanted to hurt Jermaine, could anyone believe that I would choose to do it in front of my children?

To have to respond to such allegations was absurd. I never did respond because no charges were ever filed. Jermaine, however, was only beginning to fight, and before we were through, the mud he would sling would affect everyone in the entire family.

17

With Michael's molestation case settled out of court, the way was cleared for the "Jackson Family Honors" show to be broadcast on NBC from the stage of the MGM Grand Hotel in Las Vegas. Tickets initially were sold for as much as $1,000 apiece, but in the end, seats were being given away.

Although Jermaine never paid for the damages he caused to my car, he did speak to me on the phone with some civility, chiefly because he wanted Jeremy and Jourdynn to be allowed to fly to Las Vegas to be part of the production. Their appearance came with a catch, however. Jermaine wanted them outfitted in tuxedos for the evening, at my expense. Apparently the $3.5 million in license fees which NBC had paid for the show didn't allow family members to be wardrobed.

Not wanting to deprive my children of an experience they would cherish, I dipped back into my war chest and delivered the children—tuxedos and all—in time for the program. When the show was broadcast by the network, it was a weak excuse for entertainment, filled with video clips and family footage, with few live performances. Janet appeared for the opening number and left immediately, choosing not to stay for the all-family finale, in which they sang "If You Only Believe." Michael presented awards to Berry Gordy and Elizabeth Taylor but refused to sing any solos. In his place at center stage was Jermaine, who performed "I Am the Power."

As I watched the program, I was amused to see that his backup singer/dancer was none other than Lea Bongo. The woman who came to dinner and became the houseguest-from-hell-turned-personal-assistant also seemed to have a yen for the stage. Amazing.

The show Jermaine insisted on doing—his big moment to shine as a producer—was dubbed a "celebrity dysfunction" by *Time* magazine. An article in the *Los Angeles Times* said that only $100,000 of a projected $4.5 million was raised for charity. Executive producer Gary Smith sued

Jermaine and each of the other participating family members for nonpayment of his $400,000 fee plus payments due to the cast and crew.

Despite the fact that the show apparently cost $1.2 million more to produce than it generated, the Jacksons were hardly shaving their expenses. According to the suit, there were charges for $39,000 in room service from the MGM Grand, which included $250 bottles of Dom Pérignon champagne; $30,000 for the Jacksons' wardrobe (not including my sons' tuxedos); and $7,500 for limousine service.

With the show behind him, Jermaine seemed to have a change of heart where his children were concerned. He offered to meet me for lunch to iron out the details of a support settlement. Like many things in Hollywood, however, this, too, was pure illusion. Although I agreed to meet, he never set a date. He did send flowers, though. He gave Jeremy and Jourdynn a large bouquet of flowers to give to me on Mother's Day 1994, with a photo of the two of us. On it he wrote, "We used to be one big, happy family. What happened to those days?"

I got flowers, but I got no money. Not a dime of child support was forthcoming and, after a period of waiting, my lawyers began to tighten the screws. Soon it became a war between his lawyers and mine, and for a while it looked like Jermaine was winning. He missed one court date after another. He defied the legal system at every turn. "They'll never put a Jackson in jail," he told me, flaunting his ability to escape a system that has as many holes as it has rules. "You'll never get any money from me or my family," he added matter-of-factly, forgetting that the money I wanted was *for* his family. I was asking for nothing for myself. It was to help support Jeremy and Jourdynn.

By this time Katherine, Joseph, Randy, Alijandra, Lea, and Jermaine had moved from the Hayvenhurst house to a mansion in a regal area of Los Angeles known as Beverly Park. The Hayvenhurst compound had sustained extensive damage during the January 1994 Northridge earthquake and was undergoing renovations. Michael had rented new digs for the family at the hefty sum of $40,000 a month. They were living like royalty while claiming to be penniless.

My calls to the house in Beverly Park were frequent and frantic as the weeks went by and I began to realize that Jermaine had no intention of helping his kids in any way. Finally, I appealed to Katherine.

"At least food, Katherine. He has got to help with something!" I said. I was handling the rent and the utilities but thought perhaps a few groceries could be spared in a house where Michael was paying for every carrot and peanut in the place. That day someone delivered ten grocery bags full of frozen food and left them by the door.

After months of seemingly endless court appearances and depositions with no results, the legal system finally worked in a small way. Jermaine had missed so many deadlines and court appearances that his attorneys advised him that he was about to be held in contempt. Only then did Jermaine go to Katherine and ask for money. I received a check in the amount of $20,000, with $5,000 of that going immediately to my attorneys. It was the only money Jermaine would send.

Over the course of the year, I had paid off my loans, including those to Mario, Suzanne de Passe, and Joel Katz, plus credit card debts, many of which had been run up by Jermaine. I had paid off bank loans for my children's schooling and had bought a used car. Even with this new influx of cash, I was operating nearly on empty.

I found myself in a constant battle that millions of women face each day. The process of dealing with deadbeat dads is an eye-opening experience on many levels. Legally, it's a nightmare. The cost of litigation is so prohibitive that most ex-wives spend more than they receive. When you're battling a show business dynasty, the problem magnifies itself one-hundredfold. Jermaine was able to hide behind tinted windows and iron gates, security guards and a battalion of attorneys. What you cannot see, you cannot depose; what you cannot find, you cannot serve. Yet despite all the obstacles Jermaine threw up in my path, I had two things on my side—the law and patience.

In November of 1994, I received a call from Michael Jackson's office asking me if Jeremy and Jourdynn could join Michael on a photo shoot in Chicago for his new album. It had been months since he had seen my two sons, the last time being during the "Jackson Family Honors" fiasco. The kids were excited about going away with Michael, especially because their cousins Taj, Terrell, and T.J. would also be going. I agreed that they could go—with one big condition. They had to keep up with their schoolwork.

The apartment seemed hollow without Jeremy and Jourdynn's laughter, fights, and screams of joy. They had been away before, but only for short overnight visits with their father. This was out-of-town, bigtime stuff. It had always surprised me that the Jacksons could go for weeks without calling to check on their welfare, their health, their happiness. Yet time would pass without a word. Not from Katherine, not from Joseph, and not from Jermaine. They didn't care if the kids had food, clothes, or a bed to sleep in. It was as if my children had ceased to exist.

When they were with Michael, things were different. He made certain they checked in with me every night. After Jeremy filled me in on the toy store visits, Jourdynn gave me a running account of their room at the posh Ritz-Carlton. Then it was Michael's turn to pick up the phone, and he sounded wonderful, as though he was happy with his life once again.

The photo shoot had gone well and Michael wanted to spend more time with them, so he arranged a train trip to Minneapolis via a private Amtrak coach car. With Tito's three sons on their way back to California, Jeremy and Jourdynn were alone with Michael. I knew they would be safe and well taken care of with him.

Jourdynn and Jeremy called several times during the trip, each time full of excitement. On the last call, Jourdynn complained that his uncle Michael had locked himself in his cabin and wouldn't let them in. I knew the feeling. I could imagine what it was like to be trapped with them for several days and nights on a train.

"He's meditating," Jeremy informed me. And when I asked if he knew what "meditating" meant, he said he did: "It's when Uncle Michael locks himself in his room in the dark and tells us not to make a sound." Close enough.

The most incredible detail of the trip, however, wasn't revealed until it was over. When Jeremy and Jourdynn came back home, armed with some new toys, I asked to see their schoolwork. As promised, it was completed and perfect. When I asked who helped them with their papers, they replied in unison: "Uncle Michael!"

His brother Jermaine was another story. His sons had, again, ceased to be part of his life. Even with Christmas approaching, no effort was made to contact them or buy presents. When I called and brought up the subject, I was told that Janet was sending over a truckload of presents for the kids to the Beverly Park house.

As sweet as Janet was to think of the youngest Jacksons, it didn't replace the responsibility of parents. Hazel agreed with me. She and I discussed Jermaine's lack of interest in buying gifts for his children and the danger of accepting Janet's presents. Not only would there be an excessive amount, but we had no way of knowing what Janet had bought.

Against what should have been our better

judgment, we allowed the boys to go to Beverly Park several days before Christmas and open some presents—more precisely, *two* presents each. We had agreed to put a limit on the amount of gifts the boys could open because it was before Christmas. Unfortunately, no one listened. When our kids were returned home, the car was piled high with gifts. Expensive gifts, including several that Hazel and I had already purchased for them ourselves. Once again, the Jacksons looked like heroes while Hazel and I ran around like idiots fighting the crowds of shoppers, frantically exchanging the gifts we had purchased.

I could forgive Jermaine many things, but his failure to call his children on Christmas Day was not one of them. Even worse, he didn't call Jeremy the next day, either. December 26. His birthday. New Year's Eve came and went, and within days we were celebrating again. This time, it was Jourdynn's turn for birthday cake and candles. "Isn't Daddy going to call and wish me a happy birthday?" Jourdynn asked.

I was tempted to tell them the truth: Your father is a jerk. Too self-involved to pick up the phone on his own son's birthday. A call didn't cost anything. And even if it did, Jermaine wasn't paying the bills. I picked up the phone and dialed the Beverly Park home. I told whoever answered to tell that deadbeat dad to pick up the phone and call his son and wish him a happy birthday. Jourdynn got his call and was thrilled.

The excitement of my children's world doubled when Uncle Michael invited them to visit Neverland. They weren't going to be alone, Michael said. He was going to introduce them to their new cousins and his wife of six months, Lisa Marie Presley. We had enjoyed visits to Neverland before with the children on the occasional Family Days that were held there, but it is a child's wonderland and no one enjoys it as much as the kids.

Once again, Michael saw to it that Jeremy and Jourdynn checked in via phone and the sound of their happiness warmed my heart. They had ridden the go-carts, visited the animals, watched movies, and went wild over the Sea Dragon, an amusement ride that swings in giant arcs.

Weeks later, they were still talking about the fun they had with their uncle when I received a telephone call from a writer named Ruth Robinson. I had known Ruth for quite a while and respected her integrity. It made what she had to tell me all the more difficult to hear. "I wanted to warn you, Margaret," she said. "There's a story going around that there is a videotape of Michael molesting one of your sons, and that you have the tape."

If anyone else had said those words, I would have hung up the phone. Given the long relationship I had with Ruth, however, I gave her the courtesy of a response. I told her that it wasn't true, of course, and that I wanted the story stopped in its tracks.

She had been in contact with someone who worked at the *National Enquirer* who had alerted her that a story was being written for that paper. Ruth cross-connected me with the woman, and I vehemently denied the story. Moreover, I told her that if the story ran, I would own the *National Enquirer* before the lawsuits I brought were finished. To its credit, the *National Enquirer* never ran the piece.

"Hard Copy," however, decided it would. "Hard Copy" correspondent Diane Dimond had reported that authorities were reopening the child molestation case against Michael. She had also made the allegations on L.A. radio station KABC-AM on a morning talk show hosted by Roger Barkley and Ken Minyard.

Dimond's claims were based on the word of a freelance writer named Victor Gutierrez. The story was an outrageous lie. Not one part of it was true. I'd never met the man. There was no tape. Michael never paid me for my silence. He had never molested Jeremy. Period.

One morning I learned that I had been called to testify in depositions relating to the case. A man rang my doorbell. He was carrying a box that he said was from Saks Fifth Avenue. When I asked who had sent it and he couldn't tell me, I told him to open the box and show me its contents. As it turned out, my "present" from Saks Fifth Avenue was actually a subpoena from Paramount Studios, which produces "Hard Copy." It wasn't the only legal action I unwittingly found myself in.

I was still trying to get Jermaine to live up to his legal obligations but was having no success collecting child support. My attempts had been going on for months. Finally Jermaine missed one too many court appearances and was held in contempt by the court. The news media found out a warrant had been issued for Jermaine's arrest and contacted my attorney.

On the evening newscast of February 15, 1995, Jermaine was labeled what he was and is: a deadbeat dad. When Jermaine heard the reports, he hired a new attorney, Brian Oxman, who was down at the courthouse the following morning at 8 A.M. to handle the situation.

The attorney's rap was standard stuff: Jermaine had no idea that he was behind on child support and would look into the situation immediately. According to a release from Jermaine's attorney: "Every father has the responsibility to support his children. [Jermaine] will be complying with that order."

The court case was continued, effectively giving Jermaine an official deadline to either start paying child support or show cause why he wasn't. In making an appearance before the judge, however, my attorney accomplished something else. He put Jermaine on notice by the legal system.

I couldn't help but feel frustrated by the irony of the situation. Jermaine's new attorney was being paid by Katherine Jackson. How much simpler it would have been to have used that cash to pay the child support that Jermaine legally owed.

On February 21, to celebrate my birthday, a few friends and my brother took me out to dinner. Soon after we were shown to our table, the maître d' handed me a box she said had been delivered from Michael Jackson. In front of my friends, I opened my "present" only to find a copy of a lawsuit filed by KJ Films Inc. stating that I had stolen $2 million of the company's money. On the lawsuit was a note: "It's not over 'til it's over. It is over for you, you bitch. Jermaine Jackson."

As unpleasant as that surprise was, it was more a nuisance than a real threat since both Jermaine and I knew there was no $2 million theft from KJ Films. On August 29, 1995, my attorney called to tell me that Judge Alexander Williams had threatened Jermaine's attorney with sanctions if he continued with the lawsuit. Oxman had backed down.

Far more disturbing and potentially damaging, however, was the next card Jermaine had up his sleeve. He arrived for his court date surrounded by bodyguards from the Nation of Islam, stood before the judge, and said, "I don't think Jeremy and Jourdynn are mine."

A deadbeat dad can sink no lower than Jermaine did in front of my attorneys on that day in March 1995. He denied paternity of our sons in a futile attempt to get out of paying child support. Not only did it give me renewed determination in my fight to see justice done, but it also will have a sobering effect on his relationship with Jeremy and Jourdynn if they ever learn what happened in court. Jermaine even went one step further, stating that I had been a drug addict during our entire eight-year relationship. Not only did that statement totally ignore the fact that I had been completely drug free ever since I left Tumest in 1985, it also trivialized what I had endured while I was there.

Yet Jermaine wasn't finished yet. He accused

me of beating my children. I couldn't imagine what he hoped to achieve by being so outrageously dishonest, but I knew there was no way I would allow the allegations to stand unchallenged. It was hard to believe he was doing these things to his own sons. To *my* sons. I was angry that he was going to put them through blood tests to prove their birthright. I telephoned Katherine and pleaded with her to talk some sense into Jermaine. She said she would take care of it, that he was only doing what his attorney was telling him to do. Once again she did nothing. Or nothing that worked.

After stalling for about a month, Jermaine went through with his own blood test and insisted I had to have Jeremy and Jourdynn tested as well. The procedure for establishing paternity is not a simple one. We had to drive to Long Beach to a special laboratory where both boys and I had two vials of blood drawn from our arms. My sons are petrified by ordinary needles. These needles sent them into such hysteria that it took two of us to hold them down just so that blood could be drawn.

Amelia Paterson had come along to help me. She was no longer working as Katherine's assistant, having been fired by Jermaine in still another attempt to exercise control over the conditions at the Jackson home. Despite her unfair treatment at the hands of the Jacksons, Amelia remains a woman of integrity and a source of strength.

I had told my sons that they needed to donate blood to help sick people. It was our responsibility, I said. It was a lie, but I wanted to protect them from knowing what their father had said. They were fingerprinted and photographed in an effort to maintain the highest integrity with the blood and prevent any mixup or claims that anyone other than Jeremy and Jourdynn provided the samples.

When the test results came back several days later, both boys and Jermaine matched in the ninety-ninth percentile. It was the highest match conceivable and proved that his denial of paternity was ludicrous. Not surprisingly, at his next court date he changed his story and "accepted" the two boys as his own. Still no child support, but we take our victories one at a time.

For Jermaine, life behind the protection of the Jackson gates proved useless when, in April 1995, Gary Smith succeeded in having a Los Angeles judge issue a warrant for Jermaine's arrest for failure to answer a summons in connection with Smith's "Jackson Family Honors" suit.

It's little wonder that Jermaine couldn't make time for the court. He was quite busy in April, as I was about to learn. At 7 A.M. I was awakened by his brother Randy pounding on the front door of my apartment. I didn't answer or let him in. Despite the amicable relationship I had with Randy, the only male Jackson I trust completely is Michael.

After Randy left, I phoned Hazel, afraid that perhaps someone in the family was sick or had died. It wasn't intuition; it was just common sense. Randy didn't make social calls and he was obviously upset. Ironically, Hazel was on his mind as well, for he had just arrived at her house and she put him on the phone. He said he had to speak with me, that he had something important to tell me. I already knew what it had to be. It was the only scenario that had yet to be played.

"What are you going to tell me? That Jermaine and Alijandra are sleeping together?" I guessed.

I was right on the money, almost. Randy had more news to add: Jermaine and Alijandra had gotten *married* the day before.

My first reaction was to laugh. It was the ultimate in family dysfunction. It was only after I realized Randy was devastated by his brother's action that I apologized. It was an act of betrayal that not only had left Randy emotionally wrecked, it also had put an entirely different branch on the Jackson family tree.

Randy told me that Jermaine and Alijandra had gotten married in a secret ceremony at the Hotel Bel-Air with Della Reese administering the vows. Lea learned about the marriage when she found the certificate in Jermaine's briefcase and tried to beat Jermaine with her belt, Randy said.

I was trying to figure out how I was going to explain to my children that their aunt Alijandra was now their stepmother, and their cousins Randy Jr. and Genevieve were now their stepbrother and stepsister. And their uncle Randy's girlfriend was now sleeping with their father.

In any ordinary tale of family values run amuck, this would certainly be the ultimate travesty, the climax. But this was the Jackson family, after all, and an encore was waiting in the wings.

When last heard from, Alijandra was living with her two children and Katherine and Joseph in the $40,000-a-month home Michael was renting in Beverly Park. Lea Bongo was on a trip with Jermaine to Africa, where he was busy attempting to sell yet another version of the "Jackson Family Honors" special. Maybe this time he'd get it right.

Another new face at the Jackson house is an eighteen-month-old baby named Dante, whom

Joseph brought into the family one day from Las Vegas. While no one in the family is claiming paternity, he calls Jermaine "Daddy" and Alijandra "Mommy" despite the fact that Alijandra has not recently been pregnant. Joseph remains silent on the issue.

I harbor no ill will toward the Jackson family. They were unprepared for the fame that came their way and the scrutiny that followed. Each is a product of his or her environment and upbringing.

Joseph, whose father showed him little love and was a stern disciplinarian, used the same technique with his own children. For all the animosity they now feel toward him, he did help create a financial empire known as the Jacksons and kept his family together and drug free for years.

Katherine's mother was hard-working and devoted to her children, and Katherine shows the same selflessness in dealing with her own family, even if it means turning a blind eye to their abuses of one another and those around them.

After DeeDee's death, Tito reentered his sons' lives and became a responsible father once again. Taj, Terrell, and T.J. moved back in with their dad, who is actively involved in the production of an album for their group, the Three T's. Tito was the lucky one. Thanks to the excellent job DeeDee did in raising her three boys, they are each full of love and talent.

Jackie remains the playboy of the group, while former wife Enid continues to have financial difficulties despite a lucrative alimony settlement she was awarded years ago. When Jackie heard about Jermaine's marriage to Alijandra, he commented, "Now we'll never be a group again." His observation provided a sad commentary on his inability to give up a dream that had long since died.

Marlon is still happily married to Carol, having successfully extricated himself from the family. He has a thriving career in real estate in the San Diego area.

LaToya filed for bankruptcy protection and continues to live with Jack Gordon. Through his management of her career, she can now add "stripper" to her résumé. She was driven from the stage amid a hail of beer bottles for failing to please her audience at Al's Diamond Cabaret in Reading, Pennsylvania.

Janet continues to ride the wave of her recording success and joined brother Michael in 1995 for their hit duet "Scream" on his *HIStory* album. I am among those who feel she ranks as the Queen of Pop in the music world.

Jackson Family Values

Rebbie still lives with her husband, Nathaniel, and is a devoted Jehovah's Witness. She finds great pleasure in field service, going door to door spreading the message of her religion. In Rebbie's life, God remains her captain, followed by her close love for the Jackson family.

Randy has moved out of the family home and continues to be tormented about the marriage of the mother of his two children to his older brother. He has several independent business ventures, enjoys playing classical music, and has resumed an active role in the lives of Genevieve and Randy Jr.

Jermaine continues to live at the Beverly Park estate, drives his father's Rolls-Royce, has a cook, maid, gardener, pool man, and security guard. Rather than accept available work, he prefers to live off money from his mother and brother Michael, all the while claiming he can't afford to pay a penny of child support.

The only Jackson who inquires about Jeremy and Jourdynn's welfare is Michael, the busiest Jackson of them all. He has a new album, a new wife, and his own ready-made family but has expressed a desire to help my sons. He didn't do it out of a sense of responsibility or legal commitment; he did it out of love. The King of Pop has the kindest heart of all.

Jackson Family Values

My mother, Joan, who in her youth needed to find her own way, is now an enthusiastic schoolteacher. She devotes her days to taking care of young minds and showers my own children with plenty of love and affection.

My brother, Willie, has grown into a fine fashion photographer whose work has appeared in *Vogue, Mademoiselle*, and numerous other magazines.

As for me, every day is a new challenge, filled with the responsibilities of being a single parent and forging a career for myself.

Although I dedicated this book to my sons, I want to extend that dedication to all former wives who are struggling as single parents. I urge you to make every effort to collect money designated by the court for your children. It is owed them. Don't give up.

I practice what I preach. As of this writing, the District Attorney of Los Angeles has agreed to investigate Jermaine LaJuane Jackson's criminal failure to provide child support. He will be the third Jackson brother to be pursued by the District Attorney's office for failure to provide the financial support their children are entitled to and deserve.

EPILOGUE

*From the diary of Margaret Maldonado Jackson,
May 26, 1995:*

Life changes all the time for me. The material
things I once thought were important have now
become meaningless. Motherhood and my personal and professional growth are now the focus
of my life.

Being alone for the first time has been a great
learning experience and has given me an opportunity to make an assessment of who I am and
what I want from life.

My goals are simple. I want to be the best
mother and person I can be.

As I've said, I'm not bitter about my experiences with the Jackson family. It's probably true

that what doesn't kill you makes you stronger. I feel very strong.

I'm sorry that my sons' father and the Jackson grandparents haven't spent more time with Jeremy and Jourdynn. My boys are wonderful, loving persons.

I'm also sorry that my relationship with the Jacksons continues to be so acrimonious. In spite of past history, I do wish them well.

Frankly, I'm embarrassed when my children ask me questions about their father. They say, "Mommy, when Daddy gets money, is he going to buy us a big house and take care of us?"

They understand when Daddy is not making any money. But Mom . . . I don't know. They think moms always have money. Maybe it's because that's what we want them to think.

A good mother would never let her children go hungry or be deprived of love and attention. She will do any number of things to give them the happiness they deserve.

For me, writing this book is simply one of those things.